Spearheading AI Self-Driving Cars

Practical Advances in Artificial Intelligence and Machine Learning

Dr. Lance B. Eliot, MBA, PhD

Disclaimer: This book is presented solely for educational and entertainment purposes. The author and publisher are not offering it as legal, accounting, or other professional services advice. The author and publisher make no representations or warranties of any kind and assume no liabilities of any kind with respect to the accuracy or completeness of the contents and specifically disclaim any implied warranties of merchantability or fitness of use for a particular purpose. Neither the author nor the publisher shall be held liable or responsible to any person or entity with respect to any loss or incidental or consequential damages caused, or alleged to have been caused, directly or indirectly, by the information or programs contained herein. Every company is different and the advice and strategies contained herein may not be suitable for your situation.

DEDICATION

To my incredible daughter, Lauren, and my incredible son, Michael.

Forest fortuna adiuvat (from the Latin; good fortune favors the brave).

CONTENTS

Lance B. Eliot

ACKNOWLEDGMENTS

I have been the beneficiary of advice and counsel by many friends, colleagues, family, investors, and many others. I want to thank everyone that has aided me throughout my career. I write from the heart and the head, having experienced first-hand what it means to have others around you that support you during the good times and the tough times.

To Warren Bennis, one of my doctoral advisors and ultimately a colleague, I offer my deepest thanks and appreciation, especially for his calm and insightful wisdom and support.

To Mark Stevens and his generous efforts toward funding and supporting the USC Stevens Center for Innovation.

To Lloyd Greif and the USC Lloyd Greif Center for Entrepreneurial Studies for their ongoing encouragement of founders and entrepreneurs.

To Peter Drucker, William Wang, Aaron Levie, Peter Kim, Jon Kraft, Cindy Crawford, Jenny Ming, Steve Milligan, Chis Underwood, Frank Gehry, Buzz Aldrin, Steve Forbes, Bill Thompson, Dave Dillon, Alan Fuerstman, Larry Ellison, Jim Sinegal, John Sperling, Mark Stevenson, Anand Nallathambi, Thomas Barrack, Jr., and many other innovators and leaders that I have met and gained mightily from doing so.

Thanks to Ed Trainor, Kevin Anderson, James Hickey, Wendell Jones, Ken Harris, DuWayne Peterson, Mike Brown, Jim Thornton, Abhi Beniwal, Al Biland, John Nomura, Eliot Weinman, John Desmond, and many others for their unwavering support during my career.

And most of all thanks as always to Michael and Lauren, for their ongoing support and for having seen me writing and heard much of this material during the many months involved in writing it. To their patience and willingness to listen.

INTRODUCTION

This is a book that provides the newest innovations and the latest Artificial Intelligence (AI) advances about the emerging nature of AI-based autonomous self-driving driverless cars. Via recent advances in Artificial Intelligence (AI) and Machine Learning (ML), we are nearing the day when vehicles can control themselves and will not require and nor rely upon human intervention to perform their driving tasks (or, that <u>allow</u> for human intervention, but only *require* human intervention in very limited ways).

Similar to my other related books, which I describe in a moment and list the chapters in the Appendix A of this book, I am particularly focused on those advances that pertain to self-driving cars. The phrase "autonomous vehicles" is often used to refer to any kind of vehicle, whether it is ground-based or in the air or sea, and whether it is a cargo hauling trailer truck or a conventional passenger car. Though the aspects described in this book are certainly applicable to all kinds of autonomous vehicles, I am focused more so here on cars.

Indeed, I am especially known for my role in aiding the advancement of self-driving cars, serving currently as the Executive Director of the Cybernetic Self-Driving Cars Institute.. In addition to writing software, designing and developing systems and software for self-driving cars, I also speak and write quite a bit about the topic. This book is a collection of some of my more advanced essays. For those of you that might have seen my essays posted elsewhere, I have updated them and integrated them into this book as one handy cohesive package.

You might be interested in companion books that I have written that provide additional key innovations and fundamentals about self-driving cars. Those books are entitled **"Introduction to Driverless Self-Driving Cars,"** **"Advances in AI and Autonomous Vehicles: Cybernetic Self-Driving Cars,"** **"Self-Driving Cars: "The Mother of All AI Projects,"** **"Innovation and Thought Leadership on Self-Driving Driverless Cars,"** **"New Advances in AI Autonomous Driverless Self-Driving Cars,"** and **"Autonomous Vehicle Driverless Self-Driving Cars and**

Artificial Intelligence," "Transformative Artificial Intelligence Driverless Self-Driving Cars," "Disruptive Artificial Intelligence and Driverless Self-Driving Cars, and "State-of-the-Art AI Driverless Self-Driving Cars," and "Top Trends in AI Self-Driving Cars," and "AI Innovations and Self-Driving Cars," "Crucial Advances for AI Driverless Cars," "Sociotechnical Insights and AI Driverless Cars," "Pioneering Advances for AI Driverless Cars" and "Leading Edge Trends for AI Driverless Cars," "The Cutting Edge of AI Autonomous Cars" and "The Next Wave of AI Self-Driving Cars" and "Revolutionary Innovations of AI Self-Driving Cars," and "AI Self-Driving Cars Breakthroughs," "Trailblazing Trends for AI Self-Driving Cars," "Ingenious Strides for AI Driverless Cars," "AI Self-Driving Cars Inventiveness," "Visionary Secrets of AI Driverless Cars," and "Spearheading AI Self-Driving Cars" (they are all available via Amazon). Appendix A has a listing of the chapters covered in those books.

For the introduction herein to this book, I am going to borrow my introduction from those companion books, since it does a good job of laying out the landscape of self-driving cars and my overall viewpoints on the topic. The remainder of the book is all new material that does not appear in the companion books.

INTRODUCTION TO SELF-DRIVING CARS

This is a book about self-driving cars. Someday in the future, we'll all have self-driving cars and this book will perhaps seem antiquated, but right now, we are at the forefront of the self-driving car wave. Daily news bombards us with flashes of new announcements by one car maker or another and leaves the impression that within the next few weeks or maybe months that the self-driving car will be here. A casual non-technical reader would assume from these news flashes that in fact we must be on the cusp of a true self-driving car.

Here's a real news flash: We are still quite a distance from having a true self-driving car. It is years to go before we get there.

Why is that? Because a true self-driving car is akin to a moonshot. In the same manner that getting us to the moon was an incredible feat, likewise is achieving a true self-driving car. Anybody that suggests or even brashly states that the true self-driving car is nearly here should be viewed with great skepticism. Indeed, you'll see that I often tend to use the word "hogwash" or "crock" when I assess much of the decidedly *fake news* about self-driving cars. Those of us on the inside know that what is often reported to the outside is malarkey. Few of the insiders are willing to say so. I have no such hesitation.

Indeed, I've been writing a popular blog post about self-driving cars and hitting hard on those that try to wave their hands and pretend that we are on the imminent verge of true self-driving cars. For many years, I've been known as the AI Insider. Besides writing about AI, I also develop AI software. I do what I describe. It also gives me insights into what others that are doing AI are really doing versus what it is said they are doing.

Many faithful readers had asked me to pull together my insightful short essays and put them into another book, which you are now holding.

For those of you that have been reading my essays over the years, this collection not only puts them together into one handy package, I also updated the essays and added new material. For those of you that are new to the topic of self-driving cars and AI, I hope you find these essays approachable and informative. I also tend to have a writing style with a bit of a voice, and so you'll see that I am times have a wry sense of humor and poke at conformity.

As a former professor and founder of an AI research lab, I for many years wrote in the formal language of academic writing. I published in referred journals and served as an editor for several AI journals. This writing here is not of the nature, and I have adopted a different and more informal style for these essays. That being said, I also do mention from time-to-time more rigorous material on AI and encourage you all to dig into those deeper and more formal materials if so interested.

I am also an AI practitioner. This means that I write AI software for a living. Currently, I head-up the Cybernetics Self-Driving Car Institute, where we are developing AI software for self-driving cars. I am excited to also report that my son, also a software engineer, heads-up our Cybernetics Self-Driving Car Lab. What I have helped to start, and for which he is an integral part, ultimately he will carry long into the future after I have retired. My daughter, a marketing whiz, also is integral to our efforts as head of our Marketing group. She too will carry forward the legacy now being formulated.

For those of you that are reading this book and have a penchant for writing code, you might consider taking a look at the open source code available for self-driving cars. This is a handy place to start learning how to develop AI for self-driving cars. There are also many new educational courses spring forth. There is a growing body of those wanting to learn about and develop self-driving cars, and a growing body of colleges, labs, and other avenues by which you can learn about self-driving cars.

This book will provide a foundation of aspects that I think will get you ready for those kinds of more advanced training opportunities. If you've already taken those classes, you'll likely find these essays especially interesting as they offer a perspective that I am betting few other instructors or faculty offered to you. These are challenging essays that ask you to think beyond the conventional about self-driving cars.

THE MOTHER OF ALL AI PROJECTS

In June 2017, Apple CEO Tim Cook came out and finally admitted that Apple has been working on a self-driving car. As you'll see in my essays, Apple was enmeshed in secrecy about their self-driving car efforts. We have only been able to read the tea leaves and guess at what Apple has been up to. The notion of an iCar has been floating for quite a while, and self-driving engineers and researchers have been signing tight-lipped Non-Disclosure Agreements (NDA's) to work on projects at Apple that were as shrouded in mystery as any military invasion plans might be.

Tim Cook said something that many others in the Artificial Intelligence (AI) field have been saying, namely, the creation of a self-driving car has got to be the mother of all AI projects. In other words, it is in fact a tremendous moonshot for AI. If a self-driving car can be crafted and the AI works as we hope, it means that we have made incredible strides with AI and that therefore it opens many other worlds of potential breakthrough accomplishments that AI can solve.

Is this hyperbole? Am I just trying to make AI seem like a miracle worker and so provide self-aggrandizing statements for those of us writing the AI software for self-driving cars? No, it is not hyperbole. Developing a true self-driving car is really, really, really hard to do. Let me take a moment to explain why. As a side note, I realize that the Apple CEO is known for at times uttering hyperbole, and he had previously said for example that the year 2012 was "the mother of all years," and he had said that the release of iOS 10 was "the mother of all releases" – all of which does suggest he likes to use the handy "mother of" expression. But, I assure you, in terms of true self-driving cars, he has hit the nail on the head. For sure.

When you think about a moonshot and how we got to the moon, there are some identifiable characteristics and those same aspects can be applied to creating a true self-driving car. You'll notice that I keep putting the word "true" in front of the self-driving car expression. I do so because as per my essay about the various levels of self-driving cars, there are some self-driving cars that are only somewhat of a self-driving car. The somewhat versions are ones that require a human driver to be ready to intervene. In my view, that's not a true self-driving car. A true self-driving car is one that requires no human driver intervention at all. It is a car that can entirely undertake via automation the driving task without any human driver needed. This is the essence of what is known as a Level 5 self-driving car. We are currently at the Level 2 and Level 3 mark, and not yet at Level 5.

Getting to the moon involved aspects such as having big stretch goals, incremental progress, experimentation, innovation, and so on. Let's review how this applied to the moonshot of the bygone era, and how it applies to the self-driving car moonshot of today.

Big Stretch Goal

Trying to take a human and deliver the human to the moon, and bring them back, safely, was an extremely large stretch goal at the time. No one knew whether it could be done. The technology wasn't available yet. The cost was huge. The determination would need to be fierce. Etc. To reach a Level 5 self-driving car is going to be the same. It is a big stretch goal. We can readily get to the Level 3, and we are able to see the Level 4 just up ahead, but a Level 5 is still an unknown as to if it is doable. It should eventually be doable and in the same way that we thought we'd eventually get to the moon, but when it will occur is a different story.

Incremental Progress

Getting to the moon did not happen overnight in one fell swoop. It took years and years of incremental progress to get there. Likewise for self-driving cars. Google has famously been striving to get to the Level 5, and pretty much been willing to forgo dealing with the intervening levels, but most of the other self-driving car makers are doing the incremental route. Let's get a good Level 2 and a somewhat Level 3 going. Then, let's improve the Level 3 and get a somewhat Level 4 going. Then, let's improve the Level 4 and finally arrive at a Level 5. This seems to be the prevalent way that we are going to achieve the true self-driving car.

Experimentation

You likely know that there were various experiments involved in perfecting the approach and technology to get to the moon. As per making incremental progress, we first tried to see if we could get a rocket to go into space and safety return, then put a monkey in there, then with a human, then we went all the way to the moon but didn't land, and finally we arrived at the mission that actually landed on the moon. Self-driving cars are the same way. We are doing simulations of self-driving cars. We do testing of self-driving cars on private land under controlled situations. We do testing of self-driving cars on public roadways, often having to meet regulatory requirements including for example having an engineer or equivalent in the car to take over the controls if needed. And so on. Experiments big and small are needed to figure out what works and what doesn't.

Innovation

There are already some advances in AI that are allowing us to progress toward self-driving cars. We are going to need even more advances. Innovation in all aspects of technology are going to be required to achieve a true self-driving car. By no means do we already have everything in-hand that we need to get there. Expect new inventions and new approaches, new algorithms, etc.

Setbacks

Most of the pundits are avoiding talking about potential setbacks in the progress toward self-driving cars. Getting to the moon involved many setbacks, some of which you never have heard of and were buried at the time so as to not dampen enthusiasm and funding for getting to the moon. A recurring theme in many of my included essays is that there are going to be setbacks as we try to arrive at a true self-driving car. Take a deep breath and be ready. I just hope the setbacks don't completely stop progress. I am sure that it will cause progress to alter in a manner that we've not yet seen in the self-driving car field. I liken the self-driving car of today to the excitement everyone had for Uber when it first got going. Today, we have a different view of Uber and with each passing day there are more regulations to the ride sharing business and more concerns raised. The darling child only stays a darling until finally that child acts up. It will happen the same with self-driving cars.

SELF-DRIVING CARS CHALLENGES

But what exactly makes things so hard to have a true self-driving car, you might be asking. You have seen cruise control for years and years. You've lately seen cars that can do parallel parking. You've seen YouTube videos of Tesla drivers that put their hands out the window as their car zooms along the highway, and seen to therefore be in a self-driving car. Aren't we just needing to put a few more sensors onto a car and then we'll have in-hand a true self-driving car? Nope.

Consider for a moment the nature of the driving task. We don't just let anyone at any age drive a car. Worldwide, most countries won't license a driver until the age of 18, though many do allow a learner's permit at the age of 15 or 16. Some suggest that a younger age would be physically too small to reach the controls of the car. Though this might be the case, we could easily adjust the controls to allow for younger aged and thus smaller stature. It's not their physical size that matters. It's their cognitive development that matters.

To drive a car, you need to be able to reason about the car, what the car can and cannot do. You need to know how to operate the car. You need to know about how other cars on the road drive. You need to know what is allowed in driving such as speed limits and driving within marked lanes. You need to be able to react to situations and be able to avoid getting into accidents. You need to ascertain when to hit your brakes, when to steer clear of a pedestrian, and how to keep from ramming that motorcyclist that just cut you off.

Many of us had taken courses on driving. We studied about driving and took driver training. We had to take a test and pass it to be able to drive. The point being that though most adults take the driving task for granted, and we often "mindlessly" drive our cars, there is a significant amount of cognitive effort that goes into driving a car. After a while, it becomes second nature. You don't especially think about how you drive, you just do it. But, if you watch a novice driver, say a teenager learning to drive, you suddenly realize that there is a lot more complexity to it than we seem to realize.

Furthermore, driving is a very serious task. I recall when my daughter and son first learned to drive. They are both very conscientious people. They wanted to make sure that whatever they did, they did well, and that they did not harm anyone. Every day, when you get into a car, it is probably around 4,000 pounds of hefty metal and plastics (about two tons), and it is a lethal weapon. Think about it. You drive down the street in an object that weighs two tons and with the engine it can accelerate and ram into anything you want to hit. The damage a car can inflict is very scary. Both my children were surprised that they were being given the right to maneuver this monster of a beast that could cause tremendous harm entirely by merely letting go of the steering wheel for a moment or taking your eyes off the road.

In fact, in the United States alone there are about 30,000 deaths per year by auto accidents, which is around 100 per day. Given that there are about 263 million cars in the United States, I am actually more amazed that the number of fatalities is not a lot higher. During my morning commute, I look at all the thousands of cars on the freeway around me, and I think that if all of them decided to go zombie and drive in a crazy maniac way, there would be many people dead. Somehow, incredibly, each day, most people drive relatively safely. To me, that's a miracle right there. Getting millions and millions of people to be safe and sane when behind the wheel of a two ton mobile object, it's a feat that we as a society should admire with pride.

So, hopefully you are in agreement that the driving task requires a great deal of cognition. You don't' need to be especially smart to drive a car, and we've done quite a bit to make car driving viable for even the average dolt. There isn't an IQ test that you need to take to drive a car. If you can read and write, and pass a test, you pretty much can legally drive a car. There are of course some that drive a car and are not legally permitted to do so, plus there are private areas such as farms where drivers are young, but for public roadways in the United States, you can be generally of average intelligence (or less) and be able to legally drive.

This though makes it seem like the cognitive effort must not be much. If the cognitive effort was truly hard, wouldn't we only have Einstein's that could drive a car? We have made sure to keep the driving task as simple as we can, by making the controls easy and relatively standardized, and by having roads that are relatively standardized, and so on. It is as though Disneyland has put their Autopia into the real-world, by us all as a society agreeing that roads will be a certain way, and we'll all abide by the various rules of driving.

A modest cognitive task by a human is still something that stymies AI. You certainly know that AI has been able to beat chess players and be good at other kinds of games. This type of narrow cognition is not what car driving is about. Car driving is much wider. It requires knowledge about the world, which a chess playing AI system does not need to know. The cognitive aspects of driving are on the one hand seemingly simple, but at the same time require layer upon layer of knowledge about cars, people, roads, rules, and a myriad of other "common sense" aspects. We don't have any AI systems today that have that same kind of breadth and depth of awareness and knowledge.

As revealed in my essays, the self-driving car of today is using trickery to do particular tasks. It is all very narrow in operation. Plus, it currently assumes that a human driver is ready to intervene. It is like a child that we have taught to stack blocks, but we are needed to be right there in case the child stacks them too high and they begin to fall over. AI of today is brittle, it is narrow, and it does not approach the cognitive abilities of humans. This is why the true self-driving car is somewhere out in the future.

Another aspect to the driving task is that it is not solely a mind exercise. You do need to use your senses to drive. You use your eyes a vision sensors to see the road ahead. You vision capability is like a streaming video, which your brain needs to continually analyze as you drive. Where is the road? Is there a pedestrian in the way? Is there another car ahead of you? Your senses are relying a flood of info to your brain. Self-driving cars are trying to do the same, by using cameras, radar, ultrasound, and lasers. This is an attempt at mimicking how humans have senses and sensory apparatus.

Thus, the driving task is mental and physical. You use your senses, you use your arms and legs to manipulate the controls of the car, and you use your brain to assess the sensory info and direct your limbs to act upon the controls of the car. This all happens instantly. If you've ever perhaps gotten something in your eye and only had one eye available to drive with, you suddenly realize how dependent upon vision you are. If you have a broken foot with a cast, you suddenly realize how hard it is to control the brake pedal and the accelerator. If you've taken medication and your brain is maybe sluggish, you suddenly realize how much mental strain is required to drive a car.

An AI system that plays chess only needs to be focused on playing chess. The physical aspects aren't important because usually a human moves the chess pieces or the chessboard is shown on an electronic display. Using AI for a more life-and-death task such as analyzing MRI images of patients, this again does not require physical capabilities and instead is done by examining images of bits.

Driving a car is a true life-and-death task. It is a use of AI that can easily and at any moment produce death. For those colleagues of mine that are developing this AI, as am I, we need to keep in mind the somber aspects of this. We are producing software that will have in its virtual hands the lives of the occupants of the car, and the lives of those in other nearby cars, and the lives of nearby pedestrians, etc. Chess is not usually a life-or-death matter.

Driving is all around us. Cars are everywhere. Most of today's AI applications involve only a small number of people. Or, they are behind the scenes and we as humans have other recourse if the AI messes up. AI that is driving a car at 80 miles per hour on a highway had better not mess up. The consequences are grave. Multiply this by the number of cars, if we could put magically self-driving into every car in the USA, we'd have AI running in the 263 million cars. That's a lot of AI spread around. This is AI on a massive scale that we are not doing today and that offers both promise and potential peril.

There are some that want AI for self-driving cars because they envision a world without any car accidents. They envision a world in which there is no car congestion and all cars cooperate with each other. These are wonderful utopian visions.

They are also very misleading. The adoption of self-driving cars is going to be incremental and not overnight. We cannot economically just junk all existing cars. Nor are we going to be able to affordably retrofit existing cars. It is more likely that self-driving cars will be built into new cars and that over many years of gradual replacement of existing cars that we'll see the mix of self-driving cars become substantial in the real-world.

In these essays, I have tried to offer technological insights without being overly technical in my description, and also blended the business, societal, and economic aspects too. Technologists need to consider the non-technological impacts of what they do. Non-technologists should be aware of what is being developed.

We all need to work together to collectively be prepared for the enormous disruption and transformative aspects of true self-driving cars. We all need to be involved in this mother of all AI projects.

WHAT THIS BOOK PROVIDES

What does this book provide to you? It introduces many of the key elements about self-driving cars and does so with an AI based perspective. I weave together technical and non-technical aspects, readily going from being concerned about the cognitive capabilities of the driving task and how the technology is embodying this into self-driving cars, and in the next breath I discuss the societal and economic aspects.

They are all intertwined because that's the way reality is. You cannot separate out the technology per se, and instead must consider it within the milieu of what is being invented and innovated, and do so with a mindset towards the contemporary mores and culture that shape what we are doing and what we hope to do.

WHY THIS BOOK

I wrote this book to try and bring to the public view many aspects about self-driving cars that nobody seems to be discussing.

For business leaders that are either involved in making self-driving cars or that are going to leverage self-driving cars, I hope that this book will enlighten you as to the risks involved and ways in which you should be strategizing about how to deal with those risks.

For entrepreneurs, startups and other businesses that want to enter into the self-driving car market that is emerging, I hope this book sparks your interest in doing so, and provides some sense of what might be prudent to pursue.

For researchers that study self-driving cars, I hope this book spurs your interest in the risks and safety issues of self-driving cars, and also nudges you toward conducting research on those aspects.

For students in computer science or related disciplines, I hope this book will provide you with interesting and new ideas and material, for which you might conduct research or provide some career direction insights for you.

For AI companies and high-tech companies pursuing self-driving cars, this book will hopefully broaden your view beyond just the mere coding and development needed to make self-driving cars.

For all readers, I hope that you will find the material in this book to be stimulating. Some of it will be repetitive of things you already know. But I am pretty sure that you'll also find various eureka moments whereby you'll discover a new technique or approach that you had not earlier thought of. I am also betting that there will be material that forces you to rethink some of your current practices.

I am not saying you will suddenly have an epiphany and change what you are doing. I do think though that you will reconsider or perhaps revisit what you are doing.

For anyone choosing to use this book for teaching purposes, please take a look at my suggestions for doing so, as described in the Appendix. I have found the material handy in courses that I have taught, and likewise other faculty have told me that they have found the material handy, in some cases as extended readings and in other instances as a core part of their course (depending on the nature of the class).

In my writing for this book, I have tried carefully to blend both the practitioner and the academic styles of writing. It is not as dense as is typical academic journal writing, but at the same time offers depth by going into the nuances and trade-offs of various practices.

The word "deep" is in vogue today, meaning getting deeply into a subject or topic, and so is the word "unpack" which means to tease out the underlying aspects of a subject or topic. I have sought to offer material that addresses an issue or topic by going relatively deeply into it and make sure that it is well unpacked.

Finally, in any book about AI, it is difficult to use our everyday words without having some of them be misinterpreted. Specifically, it is easy to anthropomorphize AI. When I say that an AI system "knows" something, I do not want you to construe that the AI system has sentience and "knows" in the same way that humans do. They aren't that way, as yet. I have tried to use quotes around such words from time-to-time to emphasize that the words I am using should not be misinterpreted to ascribe true human intelligence to the AI systems that we know of today. If I used quotes around all such words, the book would be very difficult to read, and so I am doing so judiciously. Please keep that in mind as you read the material, thanks.

COMPANION BOOKS

If you find this material of interest, you might enjoy these too:

1. **"Introduction to Driverless Self-Driving Cars"** by Dr. Lance Eliot
2. **"Innovation and Thought Leadership on Self-Driving Driverless Cars"** by Dr. Lance Eliot
3. **"Advances in AI and Autonomous Vehicles: Cybernetic Self-Driving Cars"** by Dr. Lance Eliot
4. **"Self-Driving Cars: The Mother of All AI Projects"** by Dr. Lance Eliot
5. **"New Advances in AI Autonomous Driverless Self-Driving Cars"** by Dr. Lance Eliot
6. **"Autonomous Vehicle Driverless Self-Driving Cars and Artificial Intelligence"** by Dr. Lance Eliot and Michael B. Eliot
7. **"Transformative Artificial Intelligence Driverless Self-Driving Cars"** by Dr. Lance Eliot
8. **"Disruptive Artificial Intelligence and Driverless Self-Driving Cars"** by Dr. Lance Eliot
9. "State-of-the-Art AI Driverless Self-Driving Cars" by Dr. Lance Eliot
10. **"Top Trends in AI Self-Driving Cars"** by Dr. Lance Eliot
11. **"AI Innovations and Self-Driving Cars"** by Dr. Lance Eliot
12. **"Crucial Advances for AI Driverless Cars"** by Dr. Lance Eliot
13. **"Sociotechnical Insights and AI Driverless Cars"** by Dr. Lance Eliot.
14. **"Pioneering Advances for AI Driverless Cars"** by Dr. Lance Eliot
15. **"Leading Edge Trends for AI Driverless Cars"** by Dr. Lance Eliot
16. **"The Cutting Edge of AI Autonomous Cars"** by Dr. Lance Eliot
17. **"The Next Wave of AI Self-Driving Cars"** by Dr. Lance Eliot
18. **"Revolutionary Innovations of AI Driverless Cars"** by Dr. Lance Eliot
19. **"AI Self-Driving Cars Breakthroughs"** by Dr. Lance Eliot
20. **"Trailblazing Trends for AI Self-Driving Cars"** by Dr. Lance Eliot
21. **"Ingenious Strides for AI Driverless Cars"** by Dr. Lance Eliot
22. **"AI Self-Driving Cars Inventiveness"** by Dr. Lance Eliot
23. **"Visionary Secrets of AI Driverless Cars"** by Dr. Lance Eliot
24. **"Spearheading AI Self-Driving Cars"** by Dr. Lance Eliot

These books are available on Amazon and at other major global booksellers.

CHAPTER 1

ELIOT FRAMEWORK FOR AI SELF-DRIVING CARS

CHAPTER 1

ELIOT FRAMEWORK FOR
AI SELF-DRIVING CARS

This chapter is a core foundational aspect for understanding AI self-driving cars and I have used this same chapter in several of my other books to introduce the reader to essential elements of this field. Once you've read this chapter, you'll be prepared to read the rest of the material since the foundational essence of the components of autonomous AI driverless self-driving cars will have been established for you.

―――――――

When I give presentations about self-driving cars and teach classes on the topic, I have found it helpful to provide a framework around which the various key elements of self-driving cars can be understood and organized (see diagram at the end of this chapter). The framework needs to be simple enough to convey the overarching elements, but at the same time not so simple that it belies the true complexity of self-driving cars. As such, I am going to describe the framework here and try to offer in a thousand words (or more!) what the framework diagram itself intends to portray.

The core elements on the diagram are numbered for ease of reference. The numbering does not suggest any kind of prioritization of the elements. Each element is crucial. Each element has a purpose, and otherwise would not be included in the framework. For some self-driving cars, a particular element might be more important or somehow distinguished in comparison to other self-driving cars.

You could even use the framework to rate a particular self-driving car, doing so by gauging how well it performs in each of the elements of the framework. I will describe each of the elements, one at a time. After doing so, I'll discuss aspects that illustrate how the elements interact and perform during the overall effort of a self-driving car.

At the Cybernetic Self-Driving Car Institute, we use the framework to keep track of what we are working on, and how we are developing software that fills in what is needed to achieve Level 5 self-driving cars.

D-01: Sensor Capture

Let's start with the one element that often gets the most attention in the press about self-driving cars, namely, the sensory devices for a self-driving car.

On the framework, the box labeled as D-01 indicates "Sensor Capture" and refers to the processes of the self-driving car that involve collecting data from the myriad of sensors that are used for a self-driving car. The types of devices typically involved are listed, such as the use of mono cameras, stereo cameras, LIDAR devices, radar systems, ultrasonic devices, GPS, IMU, and so on.

These devices are tasked with obtaining data about the status of the self-driving car and the world around it. Some of the devices are continually providing updates, while others of the devices await an indication by the self-driving car that the device is supposed to collect data. The data might be first transformed in some fashion by the device itself, or it might instead be fed directly into the sensor capture as raw data. At that point, it might be up to the sensor capture processes to do transformations on the data. This all varies depending upon the nature of the devices being used and how the devices were designed and developed.

D-02: Sensor Fusion

Imagine that your eyeballs receive visual images, your nose receives odors, your ears receive sounds, and in essence each of your distinct sensory devices is getting some form of input. The input befits the nature of the device. Likewise, for a self-driving car, the cameras provide visual images, the radar returns radar reflections, and so on.

Each device provides the data as befits what the device does.

At some point, using the analogy to humans, you need to merge together what your eyes see, what your nose smells, what your ears hear, and piece it all together into a larger sense of what the world is all about and what is happening around you. Sensor fusion is the action of taking the singular aspects from each of the devices and putting them together into a larger puzzle.

Sensor fusion is a tough task. There are some devices that might not be working at the time of the sensor capture. Or, there might some devices that are unable to report well what they have detected. Again, using a human analogy, suppose you are in a dark room and so your eyes cannot see much. At that point, you might need to rely more so on your ears and what you hear. The same is true for a self-driving car. If the cameras are obscured due to snow and sleet, it might be that the radar can provide a greater indication of what the external conditions consist of.

In the case of a self-driving car, there can be a plethora of such sensory devices. Each is reporting what it can. Each might have its difficulties. Each might have its limitations, such as how far ahead it can detect an object. All of these limitations need to be considered during the sensor fusion task.

D-03: Virtual World Model

For humans, we presumably keep in our minds a model of the world around us when we are driving a car. In your mind, you know that the car is going at say 60 miles per hour and that you are on a freeway. You have a model in your mind that your car is surrounded by other cars, and that there are lanes to the freeway. Your model is not only based on what you can see, hear, etc., but also what you know about the nature of the world. You know that at any moment that car ahead of you can smash on its brakes, or the car behind you can ram into your car, or that the truck in the next lane might swerve into your lane.

The AI of the self-driving car needs to have a virtual world model, which it then keeps updated with whatever it is receiving from the sensor fusion, which received its input from the sensor capture and the sensory devices.

D-04: System Action Plan

By having a virtual world model, the AI of the self-driving car is able to keep track of where the car is and what is happening around the car. In addition, the AI needs to determine what to do next. Should the self-driving car hit its brakes? Should the self-driving car stay in its lane or swerve into the lane to the left? Should the self-driving car accelerate or slow down?

A system action plan needs to be prepared by the AI of the self-driving car. The action plan specifies what actions should be taken. The actions need to pertain to the status of the virtual world model. Plus, the actions need to be realizable.

This realizability means that the AI cannot just assert that the self-driving car should suddenly sprout wings and fly. Instead, the AI must be bound by whatever the self-driving car can actually do, such as coming to a halt in a distance of X feet at a speed of Y miles per hour, rather than perhaps asserting that the self-driving car come to a halt in 0 feet as though it could instantaneously come to a stop while it is in motion.

D-05: Controls Activation

The system action plan is implemented by activating the controls of the car to act according to what the plan stipulates. This might mean that the accelerator control is commanded to increase the speed of the car. Or, the steering control is commanded to turn the steering wheel 30 degrees to the left or right.

One question arises as to whether or not the controls respond as they are commanded to do. In other words, suppose the AI has commanded the accelerator to increase, but for some reason it does not do so. Or, maybe it tries to do so, but the speed of the car does not increase. The controls activation feeds back into the virtual world model, and simultaneously the virtual world model is getting updated from the sensors, the sensor capture, and the sensor fusion. This allows the AI to ascertain what has taken place as a result of the controls being commanded to take some kind of action.

By the way, please keep in mind that though the diagram seems to have a linear progression to it, the reality is that these are all aspects of the self-driving car that are happening in parallel and simultaneously. The sensors are capturing data, meanwhile the sensor fusion is taking place, meanwhile the virtual model is being updated, meanwhile the system action plan is being formulated and reformulated, meanwhile the controls are being activated.

This is the same as a human being that is driving a car. They are eyeballing the road, meanwhile they are fusing in their mind the sights, sounds, etc., meanwhile their mind is updating their model of the world around them, meanwhile they are formulating an action plan of what to do, and meanwhile they are pushing their foot onto the pedals and steering the car. In the normal course of driving a car, you are doing all of these at once. I mention this so that when you look at the diagram, you will think of the boxes as processes that are all happening at the same time, and not as though only one happens and then the next.

They are shown diagrammatically in a simplistic manner to help comprehend what is taking place. You though should also realize that they are working in parallel and simultaneous with each other. This is a tough aspect in that the inter-element communications involve latency and other aspects that must be taken into account. There can be delays in one element updating and then sharing its latest status with other elements.

D-06: Automobile & CAN

Contemporary cars use various automotive electronics and a Controller Area Network (CAN) to serve as the components that underlie the driving aspects of a car. There are Electronic Control Units (ECU's) which control subsystems of the car, such as the engine, the brakes, the doors, the windows, and so on.

The elements D-01, D-02, D-03, D-04, D-05 are layered on top of the D-06, and must be aware of the nature of what the D-06 is able to do and not do.

D-07: In-Car Commands

Humans are going to be occupants in self-driving cars. In a Level 5 self-driving car, there must be some form of communication that takes place between the humans and the self-driving car. For example, I go into a self-driving car and tell it that I want to be driven over to Disneyland, and along the way I want to stop at In-and-Out Burger. The self-driving car now parses what I've said and tries to then establish a means to carry out my wishes.

In-car commands can happen at any time during a driving journey. Though my example was about an in-car command when I first got into my self-driving car, it could be that while the self-driving car is carrying out the journey that I change my mind. Perhaps after getting stuck in traffic, I tell the self-driving car to forget about getting the burgers and just head straight over to the theme park. The self-driving car needs to be alert to in-car commands throughout the journey.

D-08: V2X Communications

We will ultimately have self-driving cars communicating with each other, doing so via V2V (Vehicle-to-Vehicle) communications. We will also have self-driving cars that communicate with the roadways and other aspects of the transportation infrastructure, doing so via V2I (Vehicle-to-Infrastructure).

The variety of ways in which a self-driving car will be communicating with other cars and infrastructure is being called V2X, whereby the letter X means whatever else we identify as something that a car should or would want to communicate with. The V2X communications will be taking place simultaneous with everything else on the diagram, and those other elements will need to incorporate whatever it gleans from those V2X communications.

D-09: Deep Learning

The use of Deep Learning permeates all other aspects of the self-driving car. The AI of the self-driving car will be using deep learning to do a better job at the systems action plan, and at the controls activation, and at the sensor fusion, and so on.

Currently, the use of artificial neural networks is the most prevalent form of deep learning. Based on large swaths of data, the neural networks attempt to "learn" from the data and therefore direct the efforts of the self-driving car accordingly.

D-10: Tactical AI

Tactical AI is the element of dealing with the moment-to-moment driving of the self-driving car. Is the self-driving car staying in its lane of the freeway? Is the car responding appropriately to the controls commands? Are the sensory devices working?

For human drivers, the tactical equivalent can be seen when you watch a novice driver such as a teenager that is first driving. They are focused on the mechanics of the driving task, keeping their eye on the road while also trying to properly control the car.

D-11: Strategic AI

The Strategic AI aspects of a self-driving car are dealing with the larger picture of what the self-driving car is trying to do. If I had asked that the self-driving car take me to Disneyland, there is an overall journey map that needs to be kept and maintained.

There is an interaction between the Strategic AI and the Tactical AI. The Strategic AI is wanting to keep on the mission of the driving, while the Tactical AI is focused on the particulars underway in the driving effort. If the Tactical AI seems to wander away from the overarching mission, the Strategic AI wants to see why and get things back on track. If the Tactical AI realizes that there is something amiss on the self-driving car, it needs to alert the Strategic AI accordingly and have an adjustment to the overarching mission that is underway.

D-12: Self-Aware AI

Very few of the self-driving cars being developed are including a Self-Aware AI element, which we at the Cybernetic Self-Driving Car Institute believe is crucial to Level 5 self-driving cars.

The Self-Aware AI element is intended to watch over itself, in the sense that the AI is making sure that the AI is working as intended. Suppose you had a human driving a car, and they were starting to drive erratically. Hopefully, their own self-awareness would make them realize they themselves are driving poorly, such as perhaps starting to fall asleep after having been driving for hours on end. If you had a passenger in the car, they might be able to alert the driver if the driver is starting to do something amiss. This is exactly what the Self-Aware

AI element tries to do, it becomes the overseer of the AI, and tries to detect when the AI has become faulty or confused, and then find ways to overcome the issue.

D-13: Economic

The economic aspects of a self-driving car are not per se a technology aspect of a self-driving car, but the economics do indeed impact the nature of a self-driving car. For example, the cost of outfitting a self-driving car with every kind of possible sensory device is prohibitive, and so choices need to be made about which devices are used. And, for those sensory devices chosen, whether they would have a full set of features or a more limited set of features.

We are going to have self-driving cars that are at the low-end of a consumer cost point, and others at the high-end of a consumer cost point. You cannot expect that the self-driving car at the low-end is going to be as robust as the one at the high-end. I realize that many of the self-driving car pundits are acting as though all self-driving cars will be the same, but they won't be. Just like anything else, we are going to have self-driving cars that have a range of capabilities. Some will be better than others. Some will be safer than others. This is the way of the real-world, and so we need to be thinking about the economics aspects when considering the nature of self-driving cars.

D-14: Societal

This component encompasses the societal aspects of AI which also impacts the technology of self-driving cars. For example, the famous Trolley Problem involves what choices should a self-driving car make when faced with life-and-death matters. If the self-driving car is about to either hit a child standing in the roadway, or instead ram into a tree at the side of the road and possibly kill the humans in the self-driving car, which choice should be made?

We need to keep in mind the societal aspects will underlie the AI of the self-driving car. Whether we are aware of it explicitly or not, the AI will have embedded into it various societal assumptions.

D-15: Innovation

I included the notion of innovation into the framework because we can anticipate that whatever a self-driving car consists of, it will continue to be innovated over time. The self-driving cars coming out in the next several years will undoubtedly be different and less innovative than the versions that come out in ten years hence, and so on.

Framework Overall

For those of you that want to learn about self-driving cars, you can potentially pick a particular element and become specialized in that aspect. Some engineers are focusing on the sensory devices. Some engineers focus on the controls activation. And so on. There are specialties in each of the elements.

Researchers are likewise specializing in various aspects. For example, there are researchers that are using Deep Learning to see how best it can be used for sensor fusion. There are other researchers that are using Deep Learning to derive good System Action Plans. Some are studying how to develop AI for the Strategic aspects of the driving task, while others are focused on the Tactical aspects.

A well-prepared all-around software developer that is involved in self-driving cars should be familiar with all of the elements, at least to the degree that they know what each element does. This is important since whatever piece of the pie that the software developer works on, they need to be knowledgeable about what the other elements are doing.

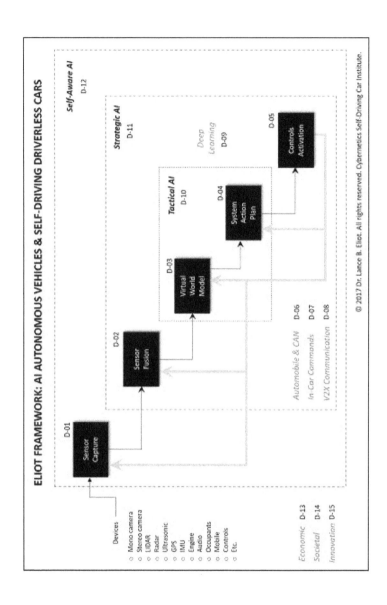

ELIOT FRAMEWORK: AI AUTONOMOUS VEHICLES & SELF-DRIVING DRIVERLESS CARS

CHAPTER 2

ARTIFICIAL PAIN
AND
AI SELF-DRIVING CARS

CHAPTER 2

ARTIFICIAL PAIN
AND AI SELF-DRIVING CARS

The word "pain" is from the Latin poena, meaning a type of penalty or punishment. The downside of pain is that, well, it is painful. Some take the viewpoint that pain is a necessity, such as William Penn's famous statement made while he was being kept in the Tower of London: "No pain, no palm; no thorns, no throne; no gall, no glory; no cross, no crown" (see his book entitled *No Cross No Crown*, published in 1669).

Today's version is the oft repeated shortened assertion that if there's no pain, there's no gain, or simply stated (with dramatic emphasis) "no pain, no gain," while some prefer to take a slightly different tack and say "no guts, no glory."

You might quibble about the no guts variation, since it subtly surfaces the notion of no pain being needed per se. It might mean that if you don't take a chance or risk at doing something then you won't be able to grab the winner's medal. In that choice of interpretation, it is not saying that you will necessarily experience pain. Instead, it is suggesting that you might need to encounter pain or maybe not, and it could be that you might skip the pain part entirely and successfully get the gain or glory. All you need is guts. This is decidedly not precisely the same as the claim that pain is apparently a requirement to accede to gain.

31

Darwin was a staunch believer that pain is a vital element to our survival, including humans and even animals. The logic he used was that pain serves as a means to forewarn when something might undermine your survival. It is a defense mechanism that gets you to respond and alerts you that something untoward is happening to you. As much as we might dislike pain, Darwin was suggesting that we'd be dead before we knew it, if we didn't have an ability to experience pain.

He had an additional corollary that those aspects that would be most likely to lead to death would be typically tied to fostering the greater pain.

If you get a tiny splinter in your finger or hand, it probably is not going to be overly painful. If you get an entire wood stake that punctures through your hand or arm, the odds are it is going to produce a lot of pain. In theory, the pain from the wood stake puncture is trying to tell you that you are heading toward death's door, while the only slight amount of pain from a splinter is a pain annoyance that you can overlook or tolerate (and you won't likely die from the splinter).

You might find of idle interest that there is a great deal of debate about the nature of pain in animals. Up until modern times, many asserted that animals could not "feel" pain in the same manner that humans do. Sure, an animal might winch and react to pain, but supposedly they were not mentally equipped to experience the feelings of pain that us thinking humans do. I'm not going to weigh into that debate herein. All I'll say is that I've had pet dogs and cats, and it certainly seemed like they could experience pain in a manner akin to how humans do. Or, was I anthropomorphizing my pets?

Anyway, let's consider that pain can be physically manifested, and it could be said that pain can also be emotionally or perhaps mentally manifested.

The physical manifestation is the most obvious occurrence of pain. Here's an example. I was moving a box filled with some aged AI books (they were from the early 2000s, yikes, stone age!), and I accidentally dropped the box onto my big toe. Yes, it was painful.

In more rigorous language, we could say that I had an unpleasant sensory experience.

A noxious stimulus occurred to my big toe.

The heavy box crushed down upon my skin, bone, and other biological elements. Various specialized nerve-type detectors relayed this impact to my overall nervous system, which relayed this signal to my brain. My brain led to a reaction that included my effort to retract my toe from being under the offending box, and my brain activated my vocal chords to let out an exclamation. I won't tell you what word I said. I apologize for the word that I uttered, though it seemed appropriate in the heat of the moment.

Notice that I carefully tried to trace the point of origin of the pain and walked it back to my brain. There is another kind of fascinating debate going on about pain, namely we might question what "pain" actually feels like and how much the brain is involved in that determination. Does your toe really experience pain? Or, is it merely reacting via sending signals that tell the brain that there is something afoot (pun!), and the brain takes the signal and makes us believe there is a thing we call pain.

I'm sure you've heard the often voiced off-hand remark made that the pain you are experiencing is only in your head. Do you think that is true or false?

Some say this is a false statement and that there is truly pain that is incurred at the physical origin point and also there is pain for wherever else the pain might spread. Others say that there is just a bio-mechanical electrical-like set of signals being transmitted and until those signals get interpreted by the brain, it's just a bunch of signals. They would claim that those signals are not what we believe to be pain and are only like electricity or water flowing through pipes.

We can pretty much agree that there are physical detectors within our bodies that are able to detect unpleasantness. I dare say everyone would agree with that assertion.

Those detectors can usually also register the amount of unpleasantness.

Prior to my dropping a weighty box onto my toe, I had the day before dropped a bottled water onto my toe (mercifully, the bottled water was less than half-full). It caused a middling of pain, briefly, which I immediately shook off, and I moments later forgot that it had even happened. Apparently, my toe was marked for bigger things to happen (the heavy box), unfortunately.

The intensity of pain can range from being quite mild to being overwhelming. In addition to the intensity level, there is also a duration aspect.

The bottled water smacking my toe was the kind of pain that was relatively mild and brief in duration. The box of books that produced pain in my misbegotten toe was relatively severe and it lasted for the remainder of the day. The box-crushing bone-battering induced pain would have been more pronounced, but I rapidly applied ice on my toe and took some over-the-counter pain relief medicine.

I earlier mentioned that pain is intended to be a survival mechanism. The pain that I had in my toe was more than just an occurrence or an event. When the box fell onto my toe, it remained there, and would have remained there were it not for the fact that I shoved it out of the way. Why did I shove the box out of the way?

I shoved away the box because the pain in my toe was telling my brain that something was causing pain, and my brain wanted to find a means to curtail the pain. The desire to curtail the pain would be due to my brain figuring that the survival of me was crucial and the pain emanating from my toe was perhaps an indicator that my life might be in jeopardy.

In that manner, the pain was a symptom. It sparked me into reacting. The reaction was intended to reduce or remove the pain. The reduction or removal of the pain could be ultimately tied to my survival. Had I let the pain continue unabated, perhaps it might be an indication that even worse pain was going to arise. The early warning provided by the toe pain was handy and helpful to me.

It is hard to be gleeful about such pain, though yes, it is doing something somewhat heroic, ensuring survival. You have to acknowledge that the pain does seem to serve a purpose. As unwelcome as it might be, it is also welcomed as a symptom that forewarns and can spur you into taking corrective action, doing so before things might get worse.

When my children were young, they did the classic action of trying to put their hands too close to a hot stove, and the radiating heat generated slight pain in their hands, so they reacted by retracting their hands. Had they somehow stood-tough and proceed to put their hands even closer to the hot stove and maybe actually tried to touch it, they most likely would have suffered third-degree burns. The earlier onset of pain at the further away position was a helpful indicator that they dare not try to get any closer.

We normally attempt to protect ourselves from pain.

This can include avoiding pain entirely, such as if I had put shoes onto my feet when I was moving the heavy box, the odds are that if the box fell onto my toe that I would have only marginally felt the blow. The pain from the heat on the stove top was a situation of a small amount of pain that the kids then reacted to avoid getting worse pain. Overall, we react to withdraw from pain when it comes upon us, and we also seek to avoid pain if we can.

There is also a "lesson learned" element about pain that boosts our survival too.

After the kids put their hands near a hot stove, they were quite cautious in the future whenever getting near to a hot stove. You could see that they had learned a lesson. The stove can be hot, very hot, so be careful when near it. Keep your hands away. Or, if you do need to put a hand there, approach cautiously. Some say that such lessons can only be learned by doing and are difficult to learn by simply being told. I assure you, I had told them to be careful around the stove, but in the end their curiosity piqued, and they wanted to see what this hot stove thing was all about.

A lesson learned that involves pain will possibly lead a thinking human into trying to avoid the pain in the future, or seek to minimize the pain if the pain will likely happen, or otherwise try to prepare to deal with the pain if there's no other course of action other than experiencing the pain. This also takes us into the realm of the infamous "no pain, no gain" claim. You might need to encounter some pain now to avoid a greater pain in the future. Either way, there's going to be pain involved.

I recall when I was a Boy Scout leader for my son's troop and we were preparing to go on a long hike in the mountains. My son and I donned our hiking boots and took a series of short hikes near our home, trying to toughen up our feet, get our bodies used to carrying heavy backpacks, and get in shape for the daunting hike. It was painful. Each time we did our short hikes, I came back aching and sore. Why would anyone in their right mind purposely do something that would cause this pain?

I did so to get ready for the major hike and knew that if I did not do the shorter hikes, involving minor bouts of pain, I'd be in for a world-of-hurt pain during the arduous mountain hike. I traded the near-term and lesser pain to avoid a much larger and far-term future pain. That's the kind of lesson learned about pain that gives rise to the "no pain, no gain" mantra.

When I was in college, I was an avid rock climber. We'd go up to Yosemite Valley from Los Angeles and do some impressive half-day, all-day, and multi-day rock climbs. One of my fellow rock climbers seemed to be nearly indifferent to pain. We'd climb for hours on end, and most of us were in pain, yet he seemed to shrug it off. At first, I thought it was a macho act, aiming to convince us that he was too manly to experience pain.

It turns out that he had a different tolerance for pain than the rest of us that were in my rock-climbing clique. I'm sure you know people that seem to be able to encounter pain that might have caused you to howl and cry, but they react in a muted way and don't seem to suffer quite as much. There are those that are on the other end of the pain spectrum, namely at the slightest bit of pain they are prone to acting as though they've had a knife jammed into their ribs.

This brings up the point that there are individual differences regarding pain.

There are also ways to try and train yourself to cope with pain. Some believe that your DNA dictates a foundational reaction to pain. From that foundation, you can then adjust it as based on training that you might do. One might argue that pain detection and reaction is a combination of nature and nurture.

Pain can occur for a split second and then disappear. It can last much longer and be persistent. Longer bouts of pain are often described as being chronic. Shorter bursts are considered acute. The chronic version does not necessarily mean that you are continuously experiencing pain. The pain could be intermittent, and yet be occurring over a longer period of time.

Recall that I had earlier indicated that pain can be a physical manifestation, and that it can be an emotional or mental manifestation.

Does a physical manifestation of pain have to result in an emotional or mental manifestation of pain?

That's a dicey question to answer. Some might say that whenever you experience physical pain, you will by necessity experience emotional or mental pain, though you can potentially control the emotional or mental aspects and thus mitigate the mental side of it.

Back to the story about the Boy Scouts and going hiking. When I went on those short hikes with my son, I wanted to project a bold image of being in stupendous shape (note, having an office job at the time kept me at my desk much of the day, and I would say that my once athletic body had become haggard). I could feel the pain from my feet and aching back, yet I suppressed any visible reaction.

My mind told my mouth to remain shut, no whining, no complaining. My mind told my feet to keep walking and my legs to keep moving.

In that respect, it seems like we can potentially mentally deal with the physical manifestation of pain. This doesn't though quite answer the question about whether physical pain can occur and completely avoid involving your emotional or mental state. Part of the problem of answering the question involves ascertaining what we mean by involving the mind.

Does a tree falling in the forest make a sound? If you have a physical manifestation of pain and it routes signals to your brain to let it know, does that constitute mental "pain" or is there only mental pain when the mind overtly recognizes the incidence of the physical pain? One might argue that the delivery of a message is not the same as reacting or acting upon the message.

Can you have emotional or mental manifestation of pain and yet not have a physical manifestation?

You are likely to right away say that of course you can have mental pain that has no origination in a physical pain. I recall a chemistry class that I took as an undergraduate in college and got a disturbingly low grade. I was in mental anguish from it! Did the chemistry professor bop me on the head, or did the grade sheet cause me to suffer a dire paper cut? No, I was in pain mentally without any physical origin.

The trick to being unsure that the answer of obviousness about whether you can have mental pain, but no physical manifestation associated with it, has to do with the brain itself. When I was mentally beating myself up about the chemistry class, you could argue that my brain must have been physically doing something. Neurons were firing and my brain was activating. There was a physical action happening.

Does my brain "hurting" constitute a physical manifestation of pain? We usually only consider our limbs and the preponderance of our body as being subject to physical pain. It seems that we usually discount that the physical elements of the brain can count toward a physical manifestation of pain.

One of the most famous cases of "brain pain" would be the so-called American Crowbar Case involving Phineas Gage. If you don't know his name or his situation, you definitely should bone-up (pun!) about him, since it's an important example used in neuroscience and cognition as a vital study of the brain (and quite related to AI).

Phineas was a railroad construction foreman. Before I tell you what happened to him, if you are squeamish then I suggest you skip the next paragraph. This is a trigger warning!

While working on the railroad in 1848, an iron rod shaped like a javelin, measuring 1 ¼ inches in diameter and over 3 feet long, rocketed into and through his head, passing through the left part of his brain and exiting out of his skull. A physician was sought right away, and within 30 minutes a medical doctor arrived. At that time, Phineas was seated in a chair outside of a hotel, and he greeted the doctor by what many consider one of the greatest understatements in medical history, in which Phineas reportedly said: "Doctor, here is business enough for you." Miraculously, Phineas lived a somewhat normal life until his death in 1860, lasting some dozen years after the astounding incident, and became a medical curiosity still discussed to this day.

In any case, I'm not going to get mired herein about the matter of whether a mental pain must also be associated with a physical pain. Let's agree for now that you can have a physical manifestation of pain, you can have a mental or emotional manifestation of pain, and you can have a combined physical-mental manifestation of pain.

The point at which you begin to feel pain is often referred to as your pain perception threshold.

The point at which you begin to react or take action due to the pain is often referred to as your pain-tolerance threshold.

As suggested earlier, different people will have differing levels of a pain perception threshold and a pain-tolerance threshold. A person's thresholds can change over time. They can vary by the nature of the pain origins. You can potentially train yourself to increase or decrease your thresholds. And so on.

I dragged you through this background about pain to introduce you to the notion of pain in the field of Artificial Intelligence (AI). I'm not talking about pain as in pain-in-the-neck and maybe being annoyed or finding it "painful" to study or make progress in AI research.

I'm referring to the use of "pain" as a form of penalty or punishment, doing so as a technique in AI.

Recall that I began by stating that the word pain comes from the Latin poena, meaning penalty or punishment. I've also pointed out that pain serves a quite useful purpose, per Darwin and others, providing us with an indicator to promote our survival. We might not like pain, and we might try to avoid it, nonetheless it does have some positive qualities as to guiding our behavior and aiding our survival.

Let's suppose you are in the process of training a robot to maneuver in a room. There are objects strewn throughout the room. The robot has cameras to act as the "eyes" of the robot. Via the images and video streaming into the cameras, the robot is using various image processing algorithms to figure out what objects are in the room, where the objects are, and so on.

If you put a human child into the room, and asked the child to navigate the room, what would the child do? A toddler might wander into objects and fall over them. I remember when my children were learning to advance from a crawling stage to a walking stage, they would often stand-up, be wobbling and unstable, take a step, and likely trip or fall over something, and plop to the ground. Ouch, they'd utter. They'd look at what they fell over, and you could see their mind calculating to avoid that object in the future.

My children did not just opt to avoid all objects. They would ascertain that some objects they could potentially crawl over and get to the other side, and then continue walking. It was at times easier and possibly faster to crawl over an object than it was for them to try and wobbly walk entirely around the object. When I urged them to go faster or made it a race to get from one side of the room to the other, they were willing to flop over an object, even if it meant getting a small ouchy, versus the no-pain approach of going around the object but taking a longer time to do so.

I bring up the toddler story to have you to take a closer examination of the robot in such a room of objects. You might assume that the robot, making use of AI techniques, would be analyzing the layout of the room, scanning visually to see where objects were, and would identify a plan of motion to avoid all of the objects. That's the Roomba kind of vacuum cleaner "robot" that does not act like humans would.

As mentioned, a human would potentially crawl over an object if it made sense to try and do so. Furthermore, the human would experience potential pain in the process of climbing up on, foraging across, and getting back down to the floor, regarding an object. From this pain, the human would "learn" that some objects are more susceptible to this crawl over method and others are not. Perhaps an object higher up is more painful when you fall down on the other side of it. The object surface such as whether it is smooth versus ragged, might also be a pain producer, and would lend itself to learning about whether crawling is a sensible idea or not on that kind of object.

In short, I am saying that at times we need to include "pain" as a factor in an AI system such as a robot that we might be trying to train to sensibly make its way in a room of objects.

Now, I'm going to get some AI sentience believers into a bit of a roar about this topic. Am I claiming that this robot is or can be made to experience pain?

Maybe in the far future we'll have robots of the type that you see in science fiction stories, ones that can "feel" pain because they have some kind of mysterious elaborated biological mechanisms that have been grafted from humans. In fact, there is research of that kind taking place today. There are special robotic gloves for example that have sensors to detect "pain" in that they detect pressure, they detect heat, and so on, trying to detect noxious stimuli that would cause a human to have pain.

I don't want to get stuck herein in the trap that this kind of "pain" is not the same as human experienced pain. It is somewhat akin to my earlier remarks about varying beliefs of whether animals can feel pain. Recall that there are some theorists that say that animals do not experience pain since animals do not have the mental prowess and intelligence that humans do.

In AI, for the time being, let's use the human meaning of "pain" to refer to a metaphorical type of "artificial pain" that we will simulate in an AI system.

Just as human pain causes a human to opt to steer clear of pain, or seek to minimize pain, or otherwise cope with pain, we can do somewhat of the same for an AI system, though doing so in a more mathematical way rather than a traditionally human biological way. We can also get the AI system to ascertain "lessons learned" by experiencing the artificial pain.

What do I mean by experiencing some kind of artificial pain?

Suppose we let the robot roam throughout the room and at first provide no indication whatsoever about how to deal with objects in the room. The robot rams into an unmovable object. The robot is stuck and cannot proceed forward. It wants to keep moving, but it cannot, as it is blocked from moving forward. The robot's Machine Learning (ML) or Deep Learning (DL) might score a "pain point" that it hit something that was unmovable. We'll make this a high number or score as a pain factor.

The robot backs away from the unmovable object. Turning to the left, the robot proceeds several feet in an open area. It comes upon a lightweight box. The robot rams into the box, which slides out of the way. In this case, the Machine Learning or Deep Learning opts to register another "pain point" though it is a low number or score since the object was readily moved and the robot was able to continue its journey.

Essentially, over time, the robot after making many trial runs throughout the room, will begin to adjust to avoiding objects that are unmovable, and have a willingness to bump into objects that are movable. This will be due to the "learning" that occurs as a result of assigning pain points. Those unmovable objects are a sizable number of pain points, and we'll setup the robot to want to reduce or minimize the number of pain points it might earn.

I've mentioned that pain came from the Latin roots for word penalty or punishment. We will apply a type of penalty function to the robot AI learning aspects. The penalties are associated with "pains" that we might define for the robot. In the case of the room, pain will be considered the ramming of objects in the room. The intensity of the pain will consist of whether the object was movable or not. If the pain is for a long duration, suppose the robot rams into a sizable object that causes a longer delay, we'll up the pain score for that object encounter.

For those of you that have dealt with the mathematics of solving constrained optimization problems, you are certainly well-familiar with the use of penalty functions. As a mathematical algorithm tries to find an optimal path, you apply some form of penalty to the steps chosen. If the optimization is getting worse, the higher the penalty score for the choice chosen. If the optimization is getting better, the less the penalty score assigned at the time.

Use chess as an example. I might opt to move my queen right away into the middle of the chessboard. This could be a great move and I am taking control of the center of the chess game. On the other hand, it might be putting my queen at great risk, right away, and I've not yet begun to battle in the chess match. If my opponent is able to quickly capture and remove my queen from the game, I'm going to be in some pain. Mental pain, one would say.

For playing chess, we can assign pain points to various moves and various chess pieces of your chess play. Whenever an AI chess playing system wants to consider a move, it will incorporate the pain related points. This could help the AI steer away from lousy moves. The pain doesn't have to deal with just the most immediate move, and could be considering future pain, such as without the queen that the AI will be at a severe disadvantage for the end-game of the chess match.

I probably should also mention the "reward" function if I am mentioning penalty types of functions. You might say that a reward function is akin to accruing "happiness" points. When I move my pawn forward, I score some reward points that I've made a move that will progress my pawn and threaten perhaps one of my opponent's chess pieces. I am normally seeking to maximize the reward or "happiness" function. Aiming to be as happy as a clam.

When I used to teach courses on AI as a university professor in computer science, I would sometimes get a puzzled look from the students and they would ask me whether they should be using a reward function or a penalty function. They got themselves into the classic binary world of assuming those two functions are mutually exclusive of each other. That's a false notion.

In our everyday world, we are continually trying to maximize our rewards and minimize our penalties. For chess playing, my moving the queen to the center of the board would get me some number of reward points. That's reassuring. It would also get me some number of penalty points. That's important since I might otherwise be blissfully lulled into assuming that my move of the queen was a rewards-only and penalty-free action.

You can further simplify this rewards versus penalty (or pain) as a formation of the "carrot or the stick" approach to doing things. Using the carrot is the rewards side. Using the stick is the penalty side. You can use just a carrot. You can use just a stick. Most of the time you are likely to employ both the carrot and the stick.

I know that some don't like referring to the penalties as a "pain" or an "artificial pain" because it perhaps gives an anthropomorphic glow to the use of a penalty function. Isn't human pain much more complex than this mathematical calculus of rewards and penalties? If so, the use of the word "pain" might overstate the power of the algorithm and the approach in an AI context.

I'd say that the counter-argument is that we are ultimately trying to get AI to become more and more intelligent in the same manner in which we consider humans to be intelligent. Do humans require the inclusion of "pain" as a mode or feature of their physical and mental manifestation in order to be intelligent beings?

If you could make the case that we could entirely strip out "pain" in all its manners, from humans, and be leftover with the same intelligence of humans that we have today, it might imply that in AI we don't need to concern ourselves with the notions and capabilities of having "pain" for our AI creations.

Another view is that maybe we ought to not be trying to model AI after the likes of humans, and that we can arrive at the equivalence of human intelligence without having to have an AI system that is like that of a human. In that case, we can potentially dispense with the inclusion of "pain" into the AI systems that we are devising.

For the moment, I'd vote that we consider trying to do what we can to model "pain" into AI systems and see how far we get by abiding by what humans seem to do regarding pain. This is merely one path. It does not preclude those that want to dispense with the "artificial pain" and opt to pursue a different course.

Furthermore, by using the word "pain" it helps to keep us grounded as to pushing further and further into how humans manifest pain and how it guides their intelligence and their behaviors. If you used the word "penalties" instead, it seems a bit muddled and less on-point that we're aiming to figure out the nature and use of "pain" and want to somehow manifest it into AI.

As I mentioned earlier, there are efforts of constructing physical "artificial pain receptors" for robots, such as the gloves that I mentioned, and otherwise outfitting a robot with ways to detect some form of "pain" depending upon how you want to define pain.

That's a physical manifestation of pain for AI systems.

We can also have a "mental" manifestation of pain for AI systems, akin to what I described earlier about the robot in the room that learns as it hits objects, or the chess playing AI that learns as it decides on chess moves.

That's a "mental" manifestation of pain for AI systems (I put the word mental into quotes to distinguish that I am not referring to the human mental but instead to an artificial or automation mental).

The two can be combined together, of course. The robot in the room might have sensors that detect when it collides with an object, the physical manifestation, which gets relayed to the AI system running the robot (the "mental" manifestation). The robot AI system then commands the robot to turn back from the object and move another way. In a crude manner, this might be akin to my children detecting the heat from the stove top and opting to move their hands away from it.

What does this have to do with AI self-driving cars?

At the Cybernetic AI Self-Driving Car Institute, we are developing AI software for self-driving cars. One aspect involves the inclusion of "artificial pain" as a means to advance the AI systems that are used to drive a self-driving car.

Allow me to elaborate.

I'd like first to clarify and introduce the notion that there are varying levels of AI self-driving cars. The topmost level is considered Level 5. A Level 5 self-driving car is one that is being driven by the AI and there is no human driver involved. For the design of Level 5 self-driving cars, the auto makers are even removing the gas pedal, brake pedal, and steering wheel, since those are contraptions used by human drivers. The Level 5 self-driving car is not being driven by a human and nor is there an expectation that a human driver will be present in the self-driving car. It's all on the shoulders of the AI to drive the car.

For self-driving cars less than a Level 5, there must be a human driver present in the car. The human driver is currently considered the responsible party for the acts of the car. The AI and the human driver are co-sharing the driving task. In spite of this co-sharing, the human is supposed to remain fully immersed into the driving task and be ready at all times to perform the driving task. I've repeatedly warned about the dangers of this co-sharing arrangement and predicted it will produce many untoward results.

Let's focus herein on the true Level 5 self-driving car. Much of the comments apply to the less than Level 5 self-driving cars too, but the fully autonomous AI self-driving car will receive the most attention in this discussion.

Here's the usual steps involved in the AI driving task:

- Sensor data collection and interpretation
- Sensor fusion
- Virtual world model updating
- AI action planning
- Car controls command issuance

Another key aspect of AI self-driving cars is that they will be driving on our roadways in the midst of human driven cars too. There are some pundits of AI self-driving cars that continually refer to a utopian world in which there are only AI self-driving cars on the public roads. Currently there are about 250+ million conventional cars in the United States alone, and those cars are not going to magically disappear or become true Level 5 AI self-driving cars overnight.

Indeed, the use of human driven cars will last for many years, likely many decades, and the advent of AI self-driving cars will occur while there are still human driven cars on the roads. This is a crucial point since this means that the AI of self-driving cars needs to be able to contend with not just other AI self-driving cars, but also contend with human driven cars.

It is easy to envision a simplistic and rather unrealistic world in which all AI self-driving cars are politely interacting with each other and being civil about roadway interactions. That's not what is going to be happening for the foreseeable future. AI self-driving cars and human driven cars will need to be able to cope with each other.

Returning to the topic of "artificial pain," let's take a look at how this approach can be used in advancing the various AI systems for AI self-driving cars.

I'll start with the perhaps the most obvious question that I am frequently asked on this topic, what in the world does "pain" have to do with driving a car?

To answer this question, let's use our earlier notion that there can be a physical manifestation of pain and a mental or emotional manifestation of pain.

For the physical manifestation, you might at first glance point out that a car does not physically experience pain. It might get dented. It might get nicked or scratched. It might get scrambled by a blow from another car. Throughout any of those physical encounters and results, we would be hard pressed to suggest that the car felt any pain per se.

The car has little to almost no built-in capability that we could convincingly argue is a pain system of some kind.

There is essentially no detection by the car that it has experienced anything akin to pain. The car does not tell you that it just got dented by a shopping cart that rolled into it. Nor does the car react to the shopping cart by emitting a bleating horn that might be saying ouch.

The car also doesn't choose to move away from the shopping cart, perhaps realizing that other shopping carts might soon descend upon the car and cause further injury or damage to the car.

Admittedly, there are some ways that you could stretch the definition of pain detection to claim that a conventional car has some means to realize that a painful moment is possibly going to occur.

Some cars have curb feelers, which I'm guessing many of you might not know what that is. These were popular for cars in the 1950's or so. They are thin springy-like poles or wires that extend from the lower base of the car and are intended to be bend and make a sound when being bent. A driver of the car would be able to use the curb feelers when trying to park a car. Upon butting up to a curb, a curb feeler would touch the curb and begin to bend as you got closer, causing the feeler to make a noise, and the driver would then realize they are getting darned close to the curb. The driver would then presumably avoid getting any closer (this was intended to for example avoid marring the white walls of a fancy tire).

In more modern times, the rise of motion sensors and sound sensors became a popular item to add into your car. People were fearful that someone might try to steal their car and by having a motion sensor or sound sensor you could detect an untoward action. This led to parked cars in parking lots that incessantly flashed their headlights on-and-off and bleated the horn until your ears couldn't take it anymore, because somebody might have innocently gotten near to such an equipped car.

Some of these systems would emit a loud voice telling you to get away from the car. This was jarring to people and often scared them needlessly. All you might be doing is parking your car next to one of these defensively equipped cars and the next thing you know that car is yelling at you. It became rather obnoxious. There were some people that delighted in purposely goading these systems to go on the defense, which they did in hopes that it might use up the person's battery and the car would end-up silent and unable to start due to a dead battery. Serves them right, some figured.

I suppose you could try to suggest that the curb feeler was an artificial pain detection device, seeking to alert you when the car was getting overly close to a curb, and you might also say that the motion sensors and sound sensors likewise were a pain detection based on the physical presence of another. This does seem a mild stretch, if not more so.

Alright, let's say that these were at best a simplistic and faraway reach of a pain detection and reaction system. Does that mean that since there hasn't been a true effort to-date to seek out an artificial pain detection and reaction system for a car that we ought not to have one?

There are some that believe future cars should have a better sensory capability to detect when something untoward might happen to the car. Perhaps there should be an outer layer of the car that can detect pressure. If someone leans onto your car or jumps on the hood, the layer would sense this action and could relay the matter to the AI system that is driving the car. This would be the same notion as the pain detection of the human body, along with the signaling transmitted to the brain, and a reaction by the brain based on the source and nature of the "pain" detected.

For an AI self-driving car, given that it will likely already be outfitted with ultrasonic, radar, LIDAR, cameras, and the like, you might not gain much by adding this kind of "pain receptors" layer to the car. By-and-large, those other sensory devices might be able to get you a detection of the same kinds of actions, doing so via their own each form of data collection.

Yet, there is an interesting case to be made that a futuristic car might be better off if it could self-sense its own woes. Did the shopping cart just cause a dent or did it bash-in the front bumper? Is that front bumper still usable? Is the front bumper now in the way of the car and might it cause other problems when the car goes into motion?

If you could have sensors throughout the car, both on an outer layer and an inner layer, it might allow the AI to be more self-aware of what the physical status of the car consists of. It seems unlikely that the other sensory devices of the AI self-driving car would be suitable to providing that kind of an indication about the physical status of the self-driving car in the same comprehensive and all-encompassing manner.

We'll next shift our attention to the mental or emotional manifestation of pain and how it might apply to an AI self-driving car.

When AI developers are crafting image processing capabilities for a self-driving car, they are often already making use of various penalty functions, which earlier I've likened to the use of "pain" as a means for guiding learning during a Machine Learning or Deep Learning system setup. A deep artificial neural network might be created via the use of a penalty function when analyzing images.

Suppose we are training a Deep Learning system to identify street signs such as stop signs and roadway caution signs. You can collect thousands of images of such signs and feed them into a large-scale neural network. The closer that the neural network gets in terms of correctly identifying a stop sign as a stop sign, you might have a reward function that increases the weights and other factors to have the DL be numerically getting boosted for doing a good job.

You might also have a penalty function. The further the neural network gets, such as mistaking a yellow caution sign for a red stop sign, the weights and other factors get deductions or penalties. These could be claimed as the "pain" for having been off-target.

There is another realm of "pain" that few AI self-driving cars are encompassing as yet, and for which holds promise as a means to boost the AI self-driving capabilities.

When a human driver is driving a car, they might feel pain when the car takes a curve too strongly or when they are driving really fast and do a rapid swerve. In self-driving cars, the use of an IMU (Intertial Measurement Unit) already provides some indications about these kinds of movements associated with the car. The AI ought to be doing more with the IMU than it does now.

This has been classified by most of the auto makers and tech firms as an "edge" problem and so it is further down on the list of matters to fully embellish.

Human drivers also anticipate pain.

One might suggest that a driver realizes that if they crash into another car or if they sideswipe a wall, it is going to cause themselves to potentially have pain. They are more likely thinking about the injury or harm that might occur to them as a driver inside the car, and the bleeding and the broken bones that would result. I'm going to lump that into the pain bucket. Those are all physical indicators for which pain is quite likely to occur.

Is a driver also worried about the cost to potentially repair a damaged car if getting into a car accident? Are they worried too about their car insurance rates going up due to an accident? Yes, and you might be willing to agree those are all "pain points" associated with getting into a car accident.

Remember we are now focusing on the mental manifestation of pain. In that case, these concerns and qualms about getting physically harmed and also getting financially harmed, you could connect to being a type of mental pain.

The mental pain therefore guides the driver toward avoiding those anticipated actions and results that might produce pain.

Let's recast this into the AI action planning aspects of a self-driving car.

The AI is trying to avoid getting the self-driving car into an accident. Why? Because the AI developers have presumably developed the AI code to do so. There might be code in the AI system that states do not run into the car ahead of you, stay back at least a car length for each 10 miles per hour, allowing for a buffer to avoid hitting the car.

Another augmented approach involves using Machine Learning and Deep Learning to guide the AI in figuring out the AI action planning. If the self-driving car gets too close to the car ahead, apply a penalty function that takes away points. Or, if you like, administer some mental pain to numerically discourage the behavior of getting overly close to the car ahead.

This also will aid in the rather untouched as-yet area of AI self-awareness for self-driving cars. Most of the AI system for self-driving cars are not anywhere close to being self-aware. I'm not trying to take us down the sentient route, and only bringing us to the notion that there needs to be a part of the AI that overlooks the AI system. We humans do the same. We overlook our own behavior, doing so to gauge and adjust as we are performing a task, such as driving a car.

Conclusion

Pain. It is key force of our existence. Songs are written about it. Most of our greatest literary works are about pain. The greatest paintings every made tend to depict pain.

Shall we exclude pain from AI systems? If so, are we potentially losing out on what might be an essential ingredient in the formation and emergence of intelligence? Some might say that pain and intelligence are inextricably connected. Darwin wants us to believe that pain is a survival mechanism and crucial to why we humans have lasted.

It pains me to say that we might indeed need to do more about pain for AI systems to further advance. The mysteries of pain in the human body are still being figured out. Likewise, we could consider how to apply whatever we do know about pain into the advancement of AI systems. For AI self-driving cars, we already use a pain-like aspect involving penalties and penalty functions. More pain might be the remedy to get us toward more human-like driving. No pain, no gain, as they say.

CHAPTER 3
STOP-AND-FRISKS
AND
AI SELF-DRIVING CARS

CHAPTER 3

STOP-AND-FRISKS
AND
AI SELF-DRIVING CARS

Have you ever looked in your rear-view mirror and watched anxiously as a police car came up behind you? I'd dare say that most of us dread such a moment. It does not mean necessarily that you are a criminal or have done anything wrong. It's the notion that the police officer can potentially pull you over, referred to as a traffic stop, which gets us nervous and on-edge. Am I doing anything wrong in my driving, you right away begin to ponder. Is there anything about my car that might spark a traffic stop, you contemplate as your mind races trying to ascertain whether you are going to get pulled over or not.

If the police car opts to go around you, it usually brings you a sense of momentary relief. Thank goodness, avoided getting stopped. For some driver's, once they realize that a police car is directly behind them, they will opt to switch lanes in hopes that the police car will merely go alongside and no longer sit behind their car. I know a few drivers that the minute they spot a police car even many cars behind them, they will right away try to maneuver into a lane that will keep them from perchance having the cops directly on their tail.

Why do police perform these ad hoc traffic stops?

In theory, the traffic stop is intended to ensure the safety of the roadways.

If you are driving in a dangerous fashion, it seems sensible that having you pulled to the side of the road might prevent you from ramming into another car or running over a pedestrian.

If your car is exhibiting some adverse condition and not fully safely drivable, suppose your exhaust pipe is hanging onto the ground and dragging along, this can create a traffic hazard for you and for other cars nearby. Probably handy to have a traffic stop to inform you about the matter and make sure that you are aware of it and take care of it.

There were an estimated 60,000 traffic stops made by police in Los Angeles last year, according to numbers released by the LAPD (Los Angeles Police Department). That's a lot of traffic stops. And that's only counting Los Angeles. Nationwide, it's estimated there are 20 million traffic stops per year. As most driver's know, a traffic stop consists of a police officer asking you to pull over your car. You are then to find a safe and reasonably soon spot to pull over, of which the police might direct you to such a spot.

I recall recently watching a cop car pull over a driver on the freeway and it was a bit of a struggle of the driver regarding knowing what to do. The car had entered into the HOV (High Occupancy Vehicle) or carpool lane, doing so illegally by crossing the line that you aren't supposed to cross, plus the driver was solo in their car and had no legal basis for getting into the car lane. A double whammy. This is a case where two wrongs do not make a right.

In any case, the third whammy was that the driver did all of this while a police car was just about four cars back of him, and one might be thankful that the cop happened to be there and that the driver was stupid enough to make the foul move at the right-time and right-place.

I say that it was the right-time and right-place because I witness drivers doing this same carpool invading stunt all the time, during my morning and evening commutes from work. I usually watch it happen in disgust and dream that somehow a police car might suddenly appear out-of-the-blue and catch these dolts.

For this driver, it was the wrong-time and wrong-place to make the dimwitted move. I was glad that it was actually the right-time and right-place since the person got caught. In case you think that I am merely wishing for ill will to other drivers, I'd like to point out that these scofflaws that enter improperly into the carpool lane are endangering them and other drivers. I'd be willing to bet that this particular driver has done this same act many times. Each occasion, his radical entry has the potential to disrupt the carpool lane traffic, and could cause a driver to swerve or hit their brakes, all of which can lead to a car accident.

When the police car quickly moved up to get behind the car, the driver must have realized they were caught red handed. I suppose for a few seconds the driver prayed that it was merely a coincidence that the police car had shimmied up to their bumper. The officer turned on his flashing light bar and used his loudspeaker to tell the driver to pull over. I do believe that there were other nearby drivers that were applauding. It was one of those gleeful moments, in spite of the usual morning bumper-to-bumper traffic woes.

The driver though did something that made no sense. He opted to rapidly slow down and was going to come to a full stop apparently in the carpool lane. Huh? Duh? The police officer got on his loudspeaker and told the driver to start cutting across the lanes toward the right side of the freeway. The police car then straddled the carpool lane and the lane to the right of it, offering a kind of traffic buffer to aid the wayward driver.

As you can guess, the traffic now was all but grinding to a halt. This one driver had managed to not only mess with the carpool lane, he now had successfully made the Los Angeles freeway traffic worse than it already was. The driver inched over in front of the police car and got into the leftmost normal lane of traffic. I was stuck just behind this stepwise effort to get the driver off the road. The police car had to straddle the next right side lane and guide the car to move into that lane. It was nearly painful to watch, one agonizingly slow lane shift at a time.

How could this person have gotten a driver's license? If they cannot make their way to the side of the road, what other driving tactics do they not know? Get this idiot off our streets, I was exclaiming inside my car.

I realize that any of us can be caught off-guard about pulling over for a traffic stop. It is nerve wracking, for sure.

I remember one time that I was driving in a rental car and had my daughter with me. A police car came up behind me, which I didn't give much attention toward since I knew that I was driving legally and could not think of any reason that I might get pulled over.

All of a sudden, and to my shock, the police car turned on its flashing lights and indicated I should pull over. I was in the left turn lane at an intersection and I had to quickly identify where I could pull over. I decided that the safest act seemed to be that I would make the left turn and then just a short distance up ahead was a gas station. I would pull into that gas station. This seemed better than trying to come to a stop in the rightmost traffic lane after completing the left turn. Didn't want to box-up traffic and also it could be dangerous to be in an active lane, since some nutty driver that's not paying attention could ram into my car or the officer's car.

I wasn't sure whether the police officer might think I was trying to make a run for it, given that I would need to drive a short distance to get to the gas station. With my imagination wildly racing, I thought that whatever had led the officer to want to pull me over might escalate into a claim that I tried to evade the police and led the officer on a car chase. Though, it would be a car chase of a quarter block and at speeds of around 10-15 miles per hour. Perhaps not the usual kind of high-speed pursuit you see on TV.

Once I pulled into the gas station, the officer came up to my driver's side window. I had rolled down my window since I assumed the officer would want to chat with me. I also had my license and also had the rental car registration ready. I had always been told that you should not make any sudden moves or reach for anything while the officer is coming up to a traffic stopped car, which could certainly make the officer nervous since you might be reaching for a weapon. I sat quietly. My daughter was puzzled and unsure too of why I had been stopped.

The officer came up and stood near to my driver's side window. He asked me if I knew why I had been stopped.

I had no idea and so I said that I was hoping he would tell me, doing so in a polite manner. Some people at times seem to confess their sins when an officer asks them this same question, and sometimes it is maybe helpful in that the officer might take sympathy upon your plight and let you proceed, or it could make the job easier for the officer in that you've essentially admitted to whatever potential illegal act that the officer suspected you performed. Others take the approach of acting like there was absolutely no reason to have been stopped and are so stubborn about it that it seems to nearly spark an argument rather than keep things cooler.

A traffic stop is considered a form of detention. The police generally have the authority via law to detain you when you are in a public place, such as the case of driving your car on public roads. These traffic stops are often referred to as a "Terry stop." That's because there was a famous Supreme Court case in 1968 involving Terry versus the state of Ohio, and it clarified aspects of the 4th Amendment of the United States Constitution about searches and seizures.

In brief, the Supreme Court ruled that an officer can conduct a stop if there are articulable facts to justify such an intrusion and when based on a "reasonable suspicion" (note that a reasonable suspicion is a lesser rigorous requirement than a "reasonable belief" which is a higher standard and involves a belief in probable cause that a criminal activity might be or has taken place).

There are all kinds of twists and turns legally about the nature of these stops. I'm not going to drag you through my own version of law school herein. Let's just for the moment agree that they happen, and whether they are legally right or not, and whether they are suitable or not, they nonetheless occur.

I had earlier posed the question as to why the police will at times undertake these ad hoc traffic stops. I had mentioned that it presumably is for the driving safety and roadway safety aspects. In addition, the police would be inclined to suggest that these can considered a valuable crime fighting technique. There are those that argue that a traffic stop can be a powerful tool toward crime suppression. It is a policing tactic that one might say is a proactive method of catching crimes before they happen or perhaps while they are happening and can prevent further criminal escalation and danger to the public at large.

I've opted to so far mention just the traffic stop part of this activity. There is also a potential part of the activity that can be referred to as the frisk. The frisk portion would be if the officer opts to not only detain a suspect, but also then perform a pat-down or other search of the suspect. Once again, I'm not going to dig herein into the legal particulars of the frisk. Instead, for the remainder of this discussion, let's assume that a traffic stop and a stop-and-frisk are one and the same, which means that there is a stop involved and there may or may not be a frisk involved.

In my personal story of having been pulled over by an officer while driving a rental car and with my daughter present, the rest of the tale is that the officer explained that my headlights were not on. It had just gotten dark about thirty minutes earlier and I did not realize that my headlights weren't on (I had been on the road only for about 5 minutes when the officer spotted my car).

In my normal everyday car, I always have the headlight sensor set to automatically turn on my headlights at night time. With this rental car, I had assumed the same setting was in place, but it turns out that the headlights were turned-off and I should have turned them on. My bad. I'd been driving from a mall and the surrounding area was well lit with street lights, and there were lots of cars around me that had their headlights on, thus, things seem reasonably well lit. It's my guess that once I had gotten to a more darkened area, it would have become apparent to me that my headlights weren't on, and I would have turned them on, sheepishly doing so and likely have put aside the matter as an inadvertent causality of using the rental car.

My daughter was as taken aback as I was that the aspect of my headlights not being on was the reason for the traffic stop.

The officer explained that it made my car a potential traffic hazard, since presumably other cars could not see my car as well without the headlights on. Plus, I could potentially not have seen the roadway fully, maybe allowing me to mistakenly run over something that I would have seen with my headlights on. He also mentioned that it is not unusual to have a drunk driver forget to turn on their headlights. Of course, he might have had other reasons in mind, but those seemed like logical and lawfully dutiful explanations.

Generally, though I am not a lawyer and do not play one on TV, it would seem that my headlights being off at nighttime would be considered a valid basis for exercising a traffic stop. According to the Department of Motor Vehicles (DMV) rules in California, the driver of a car must ensure that their headlights are on at nighttime, defined as 30 minutes after sunset and must remain on until no sooner than 30 minutes before sunrise. I probably was pretty darned close to the 30 minutes after sunset, perhaps just a few minutes or so.

Upon discussion with the officer, I asked to if it was okay for me to turn on the headlights to show that they worked, which he said to do, and he then allowed me to proceed on my way. No frisk involved. He also didn't issue a ticket, which in theory would have been plausible since clearly, I had violated the DMV headlights usage rule. Undoubtedly, I might have been able to fight such a ticket, but thankfully the officer seemingly exercised his sound judgment that a ticket in this case was not worthwhile overall in terms of a needed policing action.

I am guessing he likely paid close attention to the discussion that he and I had. If my words were slurred, or if I was unduly combative, or perhaps if my breath smelled of alcohol, I'm assuming he would have gone much further with the potential suspicion that I was maybe driving while intoxicated. In this case, he likely felt comfortable that there was no other basis for the stop, since I did not appear to be drunk, and nor was there anything else that appeared to be off-kilter, and no need to pursue the matter further.

I silently cursed to myself afterward that it was a shame that my daughter was in the car when the traffic stop happened. I didn't want her to think of me as a lawbreaker. Had it just been me in the car, I would have shrugged it off as here-and-gone. I must say that she was quite supportive and even suggested that it was handy to see how I had handled the traffic stop. We discussed the whole experience, which actually lasted only a scant maybe 5 minutes, and realized that it had lessons learned for both her and me.

On the topic of crime suppression, let's suppose that maybe I had just committed a burglary and had turned off my headlights to discretely drive away from the location of the burglary. That would be another basis for having stopped me, under the suspicion that I had been a burglar, or maybe was on my way to commit such an act. The headlights being off would be considered a pretext for stopping me, beyond which then the police might find other aspects leading to greater reasonable suspicion or reasonable belief of a crime or possible crime involved.

Using such a rationalization for the stop on that basis alone would likely have been rather weak and not especially supported by the intent and nor spirit of the law. If there had been a report of a burglary that just happened nearby, or if there was a report of a car that maybe was associated with a crime and my car matched the description, those reasons might support the stop, and potentially a stop-and-frisk. Making the mental leap that headlights off translates ergo to burglar or burglary would be a less likely scenario and a reach of the law.

Police doing policing in areas of high crime rates would say that this kind of "intense policing" can make a big difference in terms of catching criminals and nabbing gang members that are involved in criminal acts. They would tend to say that the ability of police to be able to undertake a stop, and possibly a stop-and-frisk, often detects criminals before they fully commit a worse criminal act or can serve to forewarn such criminals to not commit such acts because the odds of getting nabbed are heightened.

The downside of these stops and stop-and-frisk actions is the potential for abuses of the authority to do so. In Los Angeles, there is an ongoing and acrimonious debate about how and whom seems to be selected for these stops. Some are concerned that the basis for deciding when to undertake such a traffic enforcement action, along with the outcome of the action, might be based on factors other than the ones that are considered lawfully bona fide.

In Texas, there was an interesting recent case of a police officer that had run the plates of a car and was informed that it had a week earlier or so been involved in a drug bust. The officer followed the car for a little bit. The driver of the car apparently failed to signal for a left turn the sufficient legally required distance prior to making the turn. The officer then performed a traffic stop. Subsequently, one of the passengers made a run for it and there was a shooting involved. It was also discovered that there were illegal drugs in the car.

I bring up the case mainly to point out that the presumed basis for the stop was the failure to properly signal when making the turn. A run of the plates alone would be unlikely a sufficient basis for the stop. Now, some might say that the signal usage aspect was flimsy and an obvious and troublesome pretext to stop the car, asserting that the officer wanted to stop the car, and was seeking for any basis to do so, no matter how far a stretch it might take. There are those that worry this might be the equivalent of the movie Minority Report.

I'm not going to explore the societal tradeoffs involved in the matter of stops and stop-and-frisks. There are plentiful other avenues for that kind of assessment.

Herein, the interest is that a car is involved in these traffic stops and/or stop-and-frisks, or even a possible stop-and-arrest.

A car doesn't necessarily need to be involved in a stop, stop-and-frisk, or stop-and-arrest, since those actions can all take place while you are a pedestrian. You can be walking along and be stopped. You can be walking along and be stopped and frisked. You can be walking along and be stopped and arrested.

My focus is when a car is involved.

What does this have to do with AI self-driving cars?

At the Cybernetic AI Self-Driving Car Institute, we are developing AI software for self-driving cars. One question that sometimes comes up at conferences that I speak at involves what will happen with these kind of car stops once there are AI self-driving cars.

Allow me to offer my answer.

I'd like to first clarify and introduce the notion that there are varying levels of AI self-driving cars. The topmost level is considered Level 5. A Level 5 self-driving car is one that is being driven by the AI and there is no human driver involved. For the design of Level 5 self-driving cars, the auto makers are even removing the gas pedal, brake pedal, and steering wheel, since those are contraptions used by human drivers. The Level 5 self-driving car is not being driven by a human and nor is there an expectation that a human driver will be present in the self-driving car. It's all on the shoulders of the AI to drive the car.

For self-driving cars less than a Level 5, there must be a human driver present in the car. The human driver is currently considered the responsible party for the acts of the car. The AI and the human driver are co-sharing the driving task. In spite of this co-sharing, the human is supposed to remain fully immersed into the driving task and be ready at all times to perform the driving task. I've repeatedly warned about the dangers of this co-sharing arrangement and predicted it will produce many untoward results.

Let's focus herein on the true Level 5 self-driving car. Much of the comments apply to the less than Level 5 self-driving cars too, but the fully autonomous AI self-driving car will receive the most attention in this discussion.

Here's the usual steps involved in the AI driving task:

- Sensor data collection and interpretation

- Sensor fusion

- Virtual world model updating

- AI action planning

- Car controls command issuance

Another key aspect of AI self-driving cars is that they will be driving on our roadways in the midst of human driven cars too. There are some pundits of AI self-driving cars that continually refer to a utopian world in which there are only AI self-driving cars on the public roads. Currently there are about 250+ million conventional cars in the United States alone, and those cars are not going to magically disappear or become true Level 5 AI self-driving cars overnight.

Indeed, the use of human driven cars will last for many years, likely many decades, and the advent of AI self-driving cars will occur while there are still human driven cars on the roads. This is a crucial point since this means that the AI of self-driving cars needs to be able to contend with not just other AI self-driving cars, but also contend with human driven cars. It is easy to envision a simplistic and rather unrealistic world in which all AI self-driving cars are politely interacting with each other and being civil about roadway interactions. That's not what is going to be happening for the foreseeable future. AI self-driving cars and human driven cars will need to be able to cope with each other.

Returning to the topic at-hand, let's consider what the world be like in terms of traffic stops, stop-and-frisks, and stop-and-arrests, when we have some prevalence of AI self-driving cars.

I'll start the discussion with a claim that often is stated as though it is a fact and yet it is completely utter nonsense. Some pundits say that there will never be a need for a traffic stop ever again.

Their logic seems to be that since they assume that all AI self-driving cars will be legally driven by the AI, there is no basis for stopping an AI self-driving car. For example, my story about driving at nighttime without my headlights on, well, presumably this will never happen with an AI self-driving car because the AI will realize that the headlights need to be on at nighttime and will dutifully and without fail make sure that the headlights are indeed turned on.

That seems to settle the matter, at least in the minds of those pundits.

Wrong!

Suppose the headlights aren't functioning on an AI self-driving car. Yes, this could happen. Right now, it is unlikely to happen to AI self-driving cars because they are being pampered by the auto makers and tech firms. Today's AI self-driving cars are carefully being maintained by a special team of mechanics and engineers. They make sure these AI self-driving cars are in top shape.

Once we have a prevalence of true AI self-driving cars, meaning Level 5, will all of those AI self-driving cars really be kept in such tiptop shape? I doubt it. Let's imagine that we end-up with 250+ million AI self-driving cars in the United States alone, does it seem reasonable to expect that all 250+ million will be kept in pristine condition, all of the time, without fail? Again, I doubt it.

I realize you might try to argue that these AI self-driving cars will mainly be in fleets of ridesharing services and other such entities. Those entities will want to keep their AI self-driving cars in good working order to make sure that revenue rolls in. Any of their AI self-driving cars that might have a faltering is possibly going to mean lost revenue if it is not viable on the road and performing.

Those are certainly valid reasons to argue that AI self-driving cars will likely be kept in better shape than today's conventional cars, but it seems a larger leap to say that we won't have any on the road that perchance have something wrong with them. Any pundit that believes all AI self-driving cars will at all times and in all ways be perfectly functioning cars is living in a dream world. Not gonna happen.

I am going to therefore boldly proclaim that having headlights that are perhaps switched on but that the bulbs aren't working is a possibility for an AI self-driving car and therefore presumably a cop could pull over the self-driving car on the basis of the headlights not functioning. Now, that being said, I admit that's a bit of a stretch that the headlights are out and yet the AI doesn't know it.

Let's consider though suppose the AI does know that the headlights aren't functioning. Should it therefore refuse to drive at night? Perhaps I've driven to work and had hoped to come home before dark, but got stuck at work, and so I go out to take my AI self-driving car home and it says no-go? It refuses to drive me?

For those of you that are really strict on legality, you'd say that it should not allow you to proceed in the dark. The AI self-driving car will be a hazard to itself and other nearby cars.

I could try to counter-argue that via V2V (vehicle-to-vehicle) electronic communications, the AI of my self-driving car could communicate with other nearby AI self-driving cars and let those AI self-driving cars know that its headlights aren't functioning. It could also use V2I (vehicle-to-infrastructure) electronic communications and let the roadway infrastructure know that the headlights are out. This might allow other nearby AI self-driving cars to share their headlight beams in a sense with my self-driving car, by driving nearby it, and the roadway infrastructure might be able to adjust too.

I don't want to get mired on these points with just the whole argument based on headlights. Suppose my self-driving car has expired tags on the license plate? Suppose my self-driving car has a tail pipe that is dragging on the street?

There are various physical aspects of possible disrepair or concern that could be potentially used as a "reasonable" basis for opting to stop the AI self-driving car.

I mention these facets because the pundits that say there will never be any basis for making a traffic stop are seemingly forgetting that a self-driving car is a car. It will have various issues or failings that a car might ordinarily have. These then open the door toward a basis for a stop.

I get the idea that these pundits are focused on the expunging of presumably any illegal in-motion driving actions that a car might undertake. A human might forget to turn on their turn signal in the proper manner for making a turn. The AI is unlikely to make such a mistake. A human might be driving erratically and appear to be driving intoxicated, while presumably the AI will not do so. And so on.

I'll go along with the overall notion that much of the time the AI won't be making those kinds of human foible driving mistakes, but I've also many times expressed that we cannot assume that the AI is going to be some "perfect" driver that strictly and always unfailingly obeys traffic laws.

Suppose the car itself has an axle problem and the AI is trying to correct for it, meanwhile keeping the self-driving car driving ahead, as reasonable safe to do so, and will get the self-driving car to a repair shop after having completed getting a ridesharing passenger to their destination. The self-driving car might weave in a manner that seems like a drunk driving action.

The same goes for illegal driving acts.

There are situations whereby an AI self-driving car might perform an illegal driving act, doing so for a variety of reasons. It could be that the AI system has a system bug that when encountered causes the AI self-driving car to perform an illegal maneuver. It could be that the AI has "decided" that an illegal action is the best course of action, suppose that traffic has gotten blocked by a fire and the cars are making U-turns to go back away from the fire. If the U-turn is not legally allowed there, does this imply that the AI should not make the U-turn, even though it is a prudent course of action at the time?

There's another potential basis for opting to stop an AI self-driving car, namely because the occupants are doing something that could be construed as a basis for a stop.

Someone is in a true AI self-driving car. The AI self-driving car is driving flawlessly and fully legally. There is nothing wrong with any of the equipment on the self-driving car and it is in good shape. The passenger in the AI self-driving car holds up a gun and brandishes it at someone else in a nearby car. This is reported to the police. You might say it was a type of road rage.

Would you say that the police have a reasonable basis to stop the AI self-driving car? Many would say so.

Suppose a burglar, not me, uses an AI self-driving car to go to a neighborhood where they are going to commit a burglary. They quietly get out of the AI self-driving car and sneak into a house, stealing some jewelry and cash that they find. The thief gets back into the AI self-driving car and tells it to drive them home. The police get a report from a neighbor that saw the thief and saw the car, and believes a burglary was just committed.

Would you say that the police have a reasonable basis to stop the AI self-driving car? Many would say so.

If you think it is ridiculous for someone to consider robbing a house while using an AI self-driving car as the "getaway car," I'm not so sure that this is as farfetched as you suggest. Sure, the crook cannot readily hit the gas and try to dart away, and nor get involved in a protracted car chase. But it seems like a rather simple matter of nonchalantly using the AI self-driving car to get away.

I would even say that if you are going to believe that we will someday have only AI self-driving cars on the roads, and not any human driven cars, it seems that the thieves of this world will have no choice but to use an AI self-driving car in their act of crime. For those of you that assert that the advent of all AI self-driving cars will eliminate crime, since there is no longer a chance for a conventional getaway, I can only say that you have a completely different viewpoint of humanity than I do.

Let's try another angle on this. A person in an AI self-driving car tells the AI to take them to a certain part of downtown and proceed to wait at a street corner. The AI obeys.

At the street corner, the occupant rolls down the window and proceeds to purchase a quantity of narcotics from a drug dealer standing there. After getting the illegal drugs, the passenger tells the AI to head over to a friend's house. It turns out that the drug dealer is under watch by the police and they witness the drug buying act. They let the AI self-driving car drive some distance away, so as to not tip their hands to the drug dealer, and have an officer stop the AI self-driving car to do a drug bust.

Is this a reasonable basis to stop the AI self-driving car? Seems like it.

All in all, I'd assert that the traffic stops, stop-and-frisk, and stop-and-arrest can still take place even in light of the emergence of AI self-driving cars.

Some pundits have said that we won't need for police to ever do traffic enforcement when we have AI self-driving cars. I'd be willing to vote that it should be a lot less traffic enforcement needed, but not entirely eliminated.

Of course, as I mentioned earlier, we are going to have a mix of human driven cars and AI driven cars for quite a while, and so I'd suggest that the reduction in traffic enforcement will occur gradually, incrementally, and not somehow miraculously overnight. There will still be traffic enforcement for human driven cars, and then a lesser proportion toward AI self-driving cars, and as the self-driving cars numbers mount, and the number of human driven cars wane, the traffic enforcement volume will diminish.

Most of the low-hanging fruit of traffic stops will be unlikely available once we have a preponderance of AI self-driving cars. Catching an AI self-driving car in a rolling stop at a stop sign, not much of a chance. An AI self-driving car radically speeding over the speed limit, likely not. Other driving technicalities will generally be well-executed by AI self-driving cars and be infrequently presented for pretextual stoppage.

Would someone do a drive-by shooting while inside an AI self-driving car? Admittedly, the person doing the shooting has to be somewhat out-of-their-head to commit such a crime (in more ways than one). Besides the lack of a typical getaway effort, the odds are that the AI self-driving car would capture the entire act on its cameras and other sensors. In theory, it would be quite damning evidence against the perpetrator.

This takes us back to the drug buy instance too. By normal accounts, the AI self-driving car would video via the on-board cameras the whole scene of the drug dealer, the drug buy, and the passenger that bought the drugs. Not so good for the crooks. Though, if the passenger opts to have the AI self-driving car come to a halt, park, and turnoff the engine, this would potentially allow the crime to occur without being filmed (though some AI self-driving cars will have their cameras on at all times or be activated by various nearby activities).

I'm sure that those of a criminal bent will find a means to try and overcome the AI systems of self-driving cars and do so to more prudently perform a criminal act. It is akin to the pranking that I've mentioned in my writings and speeches, namely that humans will learn what weaknesses there are in the AI systems and be willing to exploit those weaknesses.

There are some pundits that believe there is a good chance of AI self-driving cars acting as their own form of police.

Suppose the drug buyer kept the motor running and undertook the drug buy. The AI catches the whole act via video. The AI, using its sensor analysis programs, figures out that a drug buy just happened.

The AI locks the passenger into the self-driving car so they cannot flee. The AI then using V2V or V2I calls for the closest police officer to come to the self-driving car to bust the passenger. Or, maybe the AI opts to drive the passenger to the nearest police station to turn them in.

These are societal scenarios that we as a society will need to decide how to best deal with. Are we willing or wanting to have the AI be examining the sensory data for these kinds of illegal acts? If so, does this provide a slippery slope toward a Big Brother kind of atmosphere that we will all be subject to?

This also raises the question of the AI self-driving car as a kind of tattletale. Will the massive amount of sensory data being collected by the AI for purposes of driving the car be used for other purposes? Some of the data will be stored in the on-board AI systems and some of it will be stored in the cloud. Does the location of the data make a difference as to what is discoverable versus what is not?

There are already byzantine laws about what, where, how, and why the search of a car can be undertaken. The added twist for AI self-driving cars is that a lot more data will be recorded and kept, more so than on conventional cars. It will be an arduous effort of the courts and the legislature to ultimately figure out what is the proper balance between the data being private versus considered usable for crime fighting efforts.

Speaking of a tattletale, suppose the drug buy has happened and the AI self-driving car is heading to the friend's house that the passenger wants to go visit. The friend's house is staked out by the police, as they've gotten a tip that it is a place where there is a lot of illegal drugs being used.

The AI self-driving car comes down the street and a police officer stops the self-driving car. The officer goes to the window to speak with the passenger. Do you have any illegal drugs in there, the officer asks? The passenger says no. The AI, listening to the conversation, speaks up and says that there are illegal drugs and that the passenger had minutes earlier made a buy. Wham, the passenger is busted!

If you don't like that scenario, here's a different one.

The passenger says no, they don't have any illegal drugs. The AI, listening to the conversation, speaks up and tells the officer that there was no basis for the traffic stop. Furthermore, the AI advises the passenger to not say anything else to the officer and to refuse any entry into the self-driving car by the officer. In that manner, the AI is acting like a legal advisor to the passenger. The passenger has purposely purchased an add-on to the AI self-driving car system that would aid him in the case of any traffic stops.

That's a bit of a twist!

I'll add some additional twists that you might find of interest.

Roadblocks and sobriety checkpoints are generally legally allowed junctures at which you can be stopped while in your car. It is presumed that there is already a defacto kind of reasonable suspicion to stop your car.

Will being inside an AI self-driving car impact those legal stops?

If there isn't a human driver, one might assert that the AI self-driving car should not need to stop at a sobriety checkpoint. For a roadblock of another kind, there is not necessarily that same get-out-of-jail free card.

Okay, that was interesting, what about this one. An AI self-driving car has no passengers in it. Someone wanting to buy some drugs sends the AI self-driving car to that street corner where the drug dealer hangs out. The AI self-driving car halts at the street corner. The drug buyer is on a smartphone and tells the drug dealer to go ahead and toss the drugs into the self-driving car and meanwhile remotely the drug buyer rolls down the window. The drug dealer tosses in the drugs and at the same time bitcoins are sent to the drug dealer to cover the cost of the drug buy.

The police were watching the drug dealer. They see the AI self-driving car drive away after making the drug buy. Can the police stop the AI self-driving car? If they do, and they find the drugs, is that sufficient to try and go find the buyer and bust that person?

Conclusion

A future of all and only AI self-driving cars is a long way off. We have time to be considering how our society might be changed by the advent of AI self-driving cars.

I've tried to make the case that we are still going to have traffic stops, along with stop-and-frisks and stop-and-arrests. This certainly will last as long as we also have conventional cars or at least AI self-driving cars less than a Level 5. Even once we have Level 5 AI self-driving cars, there are still many opportunities to potentially do a traffic stop.

It would be nice to think that the advent of AI self-driving cars would magically curtail crime because the use of an AI self-driving car as your "accessory to the crime" as being your getaway driver is seemingly impractical. Nonetheless, there is still sadly opportunity to commit crimes, involving the use of AI self-driving cars, and it is as much a societal question as a systems AI question.

CHAPTER 4

CARS CAREENING
AND
AI SELF-DRIVING CARS

CHAPTER 4

CARS CAREENING
AND AI SELF-DRIVING CARS

Bam! While innocently sitting at a red light, a car rammed into the rear of my car. I was not expecting it. Things began to happen so quickly that I barely remember what actually did happen once the crash began.

Within just a few brisk seconds, my car got pushed into a car ahead of me, my car got ripped-up along the back and left-side of my car, the gas tank ruptured and gasoline leaked onto the ground, my airbag deployed, most of the windows of the car fractured and bits of glass flew everywhere, and basically all heck broke loose.

This actually happened to me some years ago when I was a university professor. I had been driving past a senior citizens home on my way to the campus. A car driven by someone quite elderly had come up behind me at the red light and he inadvertently punched on the accelerator rather than the brake. His action then rammed his car into my car, and my car rammed into the car ahead of me. Fortunately, I survived with hardly any injuries, and nor was the elderly driver particularly injured, nor the driver in the car ahead of me was injured.

If you saw a picture of my car after the incident, you'd believe that no one in my car should or could have survived the crash. My car was totaled. I think back to that crash and can readily talk about it today, but at the time it was quite a shocker.

Speaking of shock, I am pretty sure that I must have temporarily gone into shock when the crash first started. I say this because I really do not remember exactly how things went in those few life-threatening seconds. All I can remember is that I kind of "woke-up" in that I consciously realized the air bag had deployed, and that my windshield was busted, otherwise I was utterly confused about what was going on. It was as though a magic wand had transformed my setting into some other bizarre world.

As I sat there in the driver's seat looking stunned, and as I slowly looked around to survey the scene, trying to make sense of what had just occurred, some people from other cars nearby had gotten out of their cars right away and ran to my car. With my driver's side window nearly entirely smashed and gone, they yelled into the car and asked me if I was okay. I looked at them and wasn't sure that I understood what they were asking me and nor why they were even talking to me.

It was at that point that I smelled the heavy odor of gasoline. In that same instant, the people standing outside my driver's side window were yelling for me to get out of the car because of the gasoline that had poured onto the street. I realized later on that these good Samaritans were very brave and generous to have endangered themselves in order to warn me about the dangers that I faced.

Luckily the car door still worked, so I opened it, undid my seat belt, pushed away the remains of the air bag, shifted my body and my legs to position outside the door, and stepped out of the car. I nearly collapsed. Turns out my legs had gone weak as the aftermath of the shock and fright involved. Several people helped walk and semi-drag me to the curb and get away from the car itself. I sat there on the curb, watching as everyone was running around trying to help, and for a moment I thought it had occurred without me being involved at all. I was just a bystander sitting at the curb after a car accident had happened.

When the police and an ambulance showed-up, I had regained my composure. I was standing up sturdily now and calmly examining the cars. At first, the police officers and the medical crew doubted that I had been inside the car and certainly doubted that I had been the driver. I had nary a scratch on me. I seemed coherent and able to talk about what had happened.

In fact, and you'll maybe laugh at this, I was mainly worried that I would be late to teach my class at the college. I had never been late to any of my lectures. What would the students do, what would they think? Of course, I realized later on, after several years of being a professor, the students probably welcomed being able to skip a lecture and would fruitfully use their time for other "academic" purposes.

The main aspect about the incident was that my mind was blurry about those key seconds between having gotten hit from behind and the realization that I was sitting in my driver's seat and glass was around me and my airbag was in front of me. I cannot to this day tell you exactly what happened in those precious few seconds.

I am pretty sure that my body was likely a rag doll and merely flopped around as the impact to the car occurred.

Which way was my head facing? Well, I had been looking straight ahead at the intersection while waiting for a green light, so presumably my head was still pointed in that direction when the initial impact occurred. Where were my arms and hands? I had been lightly holding the steering wheel and so that's where my arms and hands were, at least up until the impact. My legs and feet were under the dash and positioned at the pedals, including that my right foot was on the brake, doing so because I was at a red light and stopped, again that was just before the impact.

I wondered whether there was anything I could have done once the impact began.

Suppose I had been forewarned and told or knew that a car was going to violently ram into the back of my car. Let's further assume that I didn't have sufficient time to get out of the way or make any kind of evasive maneuver.

It's an interesting problem to postulate.

We usually think about the ways to avoid a car accident.

In this case, if I had some premonition or clue that the accident was going to happen, maybe I could have tried to turn the wheels of the car so that it might move away from the car ahead of me once my car got rammed. Or, maybe I might have put on the parking brake in hopes it would further keep my car from being pushed by the ramming action.

The medics at the scene told me that I was probably lucky that I did not realize that the ramming was going to occur, since most people tense up.

They said that tensing up is often worse for you when you get into a car accident. According to their medical training and experience, there is a greater chance that when being jarred harshly, jostled and tossed around, the tightened or tensed muscles of my body would try to fight against the movement, and likely lose, thus it would lead to greater physical injury to my body. Instead, by being loose and unknowing, my body was more fluid and accommodated the rapid pushing, shoving, and fierce shaking.

I'd like to though put aside the idea that I might have been forewarned, and instead consider a slightly different angle to the incident. Suppose that my mind had remained clearly alert and available during those few seconds in which the accident evolved. I mentioned to you earlier that I have no particular recall and those moments are blurry in my mind, let's pretend differently.

Pretend that my mind was completely untouched and could act as though it was separate from the severe contortions happening to my physical body. What then?

We'll start the clock at the moment of impact. The car behind me has just collided into the rear of my car. This is time zero. Over the next few seconds, the impact will work its way throughout my car. You might want to consider this akin to those popular online videos in which things are filmed in slow motion. You know, the videos that show what it looks like in the split seconds of a bullet going through a piece of wood or a watermelon being smashed. Imagine a slow-motion version of my car incident.

We're now assuming that my mind can undertake whatever kind of thinking might be pertinent to the matter at-hand. Of course, my mind might be thinking about that lecture I was going to give that day, or maybe what I was going to eat for dinner that night. Put those thoughts aside. In this slow-motion version, devote my mind to focusing on the car accident that is happening.

I'd also suggest that we assume that my senses are all in perfect working order too. You might argue that my senses are going to get muddled by the forceful jerking efforts of the car being rammed, which I agree seems likely. In a moment, I'll revisit the pretend with that mushing effect to my senses as another variation.

Okay, my mind is fully active, focused on the car incident as the clock starts to tick, and I've got control over my sensory faculties and we'll include that I have control over my body. This means that I can take whatever kind of driving action that I want to undertake. Is there anything that I can do to drive the car in those few seconds that might in some manner lessen the impacts of the car accident?

Maybe I had taken my foot off the brakes when the real accident occurred, reflexively, and in the case of this pretend we could assert that I am going to keep my foot on the brakes. Perhaps my arms and hands flew off the steering wheel in the real incident. Let's pretend that I keep them on the steering wheel.

It's not evident how much my added ability to control the car in this particular incident is going to be aided by my clear mind and the use of my senses and my body.

One limiting factor is the car and the circumstances of where the car was positioned. The car was being pushed fiercely from behind. In this case, the brakes weren't doing much in those split seconds anyway. The fact that there was a car ahead of me pretty much stopped my car from going much further ahead, due to my ramming into it and I was pinned between two cars now. One car pushing from behind, the other car at a standstill and preventing me from readily driving forward.

The car itself is a limiting factor too in that the brakes might have gotten cut anyway upon the impact to the car. In that case, pushing on the brake pedal might not have had any material effect. Likewise, the steering wheel might not be useful during those few seconds, if the linkages and internal steering controls were damaged or unable to relay my positioning of the steering wheel.

In my case, I'm going to toss in the towel and say that it is unlikely that if my mind had remained clear and available, and if my senses were continually available and working, and if my body was functioning so that I could use it to actively and purposely drive the car, there's not much that could have gone differently to improve what happened during those seconds of impact and reaction.

If you look at different circumstances, the results might come out differently.

Remove the car that was ahead of me. Pretend I have a straight-ahead path. Assume too that I can see the intersection and there's no cars in it, meaning that I can use the intersection if I want to do so. Does this change things?

In theory, depending upon the pace at which my car can accelerate, and depending upon the pace at which the car from behind me is ramming into me, there is some chance that I could have punched down on the accelerator and tried to leap ahead. It would have become a kind of race, starting when the impact began, the zero-clock point that I mentioned earlier. This could potentially have allowed me to lessen the blow from the rear of my car. I might even have accelerated fast enough to escape much of the impact, ending up on the other side of the intersection without much damage to the rear of my car.

I'd bet there are many car accidents wherein if the driver involved could magically have a clear and present mind, and be able to control their car, there is a chance that whatever dire results occurred could have been lessened.

On the news, I saw an instance recently of a driver that veered their car to avoid hitting something in the street and the car driver lost control of the car, which resulted in the car ramming into a parked car and a light post and a fire hydrant. It sheered off the fire hydrant and sent water shooting into the sky.

How did the driver lose control of the car?

Was it because of the mechanics of the car, or was it because the driver themselves lost their presence of mind and no longer were of their right mental faculties? It could be that the shock of veering caused the person to mentally go into a blur. This blurred mental state meant that the human was no longer actively driving the car. The car was out-of-control. There was no driver actively driving the car.

I'm sure you've seen lots of news clips and videos of cars that became a kind of mindless projectile.

There was an incident captured on YouTube of a car that swerved to avoid hitting an animal in the street and the car smashed through a wood fence, continued onto a farm adjacent to the road, plowed a bunch of planted vegetables, and finally the car came to a stop. Out-of-control car.

Another incident showed a car that didn't make a left turn very well, veering beyond the confines of the left turn. The car continued to make too large a turn and rammed into a mailbox. This car then rammed into a hot dog vendor stand and ultimately came to a stop once it hit a storefront.

There are plenty of videos of cars that missed a turn and went through a fence into someone's swimming pool. Having a car fly off a bridge is another example of an out-of-control car.

There are situations whereby an out-of-control car might be due to the car having mechanical problems and there is seemingly nothing that the driver can potentially do. For example, the accelerator pedal getting stuck and refusing to budge, forcing the car into going faster and faster. This might happen because something is lodged into the accelerator pedal like a floor mat. It has also happened as a result of an intrinsic defect in the car design.

Assume that the driver did not cause the accelerator pedal to be jammed downward. In that instance, is the driver now merely a passenger in that there is nothing the driver can do? I'd dare say we would all agree that the driver can still do something. They need to try and steer the car to avoid hitting other cars and other objects. They could try to see if they could dislodge the pedal to curtail the rapid acceleration. They could start honking their horn to try and warn other drivers and pedestrians that the car is a runaway. And so on.

Not everyone would have the presence of mind to do those things. If you've never had your accelerator pedal get stuck, the odds are that when it does get stuck, you'll be shocked and unsure of what to do. You might lose your mental presence and become panicked. Even though there are actions you could take, those actions might not come to your mind. If they do come to your mind, you'd have to remain calm enough to enact those actions by forcing your body to undertake the desired actions.

Have you ever been to a demolition derby or seen one on TV? At a demolition derby, the cars all try to smash into each other. It's the purpose for the derby. Usually, the last running car gets the grand prize. I bring up the topic of demolition derbies to point out that those drivers are well-prepared to deal with their cars when the car is out-of-control.

A driver in one car might get hit from the left side by another car, meanwhile be getting hit from the right side by another car, and at the same time trying to hit a car ahead of them. The cars are all being pushed and shoved. Driver's in those cars are generally able to keep their mind and wits about them. They are trained for the situation and know what to do, though of course it is somewhat easier when the matter is expected versus when unexpected (in the derby, it is expected that your car is going to be hit and go out-of-control).

One aspect of a car being out-of-control is when the car is sliding or otherwise in a motion that you as a driver did not intentionally seek to have the car do. Have you ever had your car slide on ice or snow? That's an example of the car being out-of-control.

Again, how you react as the driver can make a big difference. If you aren't aware of the sliding action and aren't prepared to react, or if your mind is muddled, you might not try the usual techniques that are recommended for dealing with a sliding car. You can potentially regain control by typically turning the wheels in the direction of the slide and avoid jamming on the brakes.

In essence, there are actions that you can take to bring the car back into control, or you can take no actions and hope for the best, or you can take misguided actions that cause the car to go into a further out-of-control result.

You need to not only determine what is the proper course of action, you need to try and prevent the situation from getting worse, you need to take into account what your car can and cannot do, you need to consider any damage the car is undertaking and how it will limit what you can do, and consider a slew of other factors.

Demolition derby drivers are able to do this. I don't want to make them into seeming to be super drivers per se. Their cars are usually jiggered in a manner to make things simpler for them. Usually, the cars are stripped of items that can fly around. Cables are reinforced. There aren't any passengers on-board. Gas tanks get special protections. Plus, the derby typically takes place in a confined area that has no pedestrians, no other obstacles, and it is like a playground in which all you can do is ram into other cars.

That's a far cry from dealing with a real-world crash-mode and having to figure out what to do, and cope with bystanders, and cope with a myriad of other factors. Nonetheless, the derby drivers get a chance to practice dealing with the stresses of being in a car crash and able to train themselves to keep a mental awareness, enabling them to continue driving a car and maintain control, as much as feasible.

What does this have to do with AI self-driving cars?

At the Cybernetic AI Self-Driving Car Institute, we are developing AI software for self-driving cars. One aspect that few auto makers and tech firms are considering at this time is the special characteristics of driving a car while it is in crash-mode and how the AI should be skilled to do so.

Allow me to elaborate.

I'd like to first clarify and introduce the notion that there are varying levels of AI self-driving cars. The topmost level is considered Level 5. A Level 5 self-driving car is one that is being driven by the AI and there is no human driver involved. For the design of Level 5 self-driving cars, the auto makers are even removing the gas pedal, brake pedal, and steering wheel, since those are contraptions used by human drivers. The Level 5 self-driving car is not being driven by a human and nor is there an expectation that a human driver will be present in the self-driving car. It's all on the shoulders of the AI to drive the car.

For self-driving cars less than a Level 5, there must be a human driver present in the car. The human driver is currently considered the responsible party for the acts of the car. The AI and the human driver are co-sharing the driving task. In spite of this co-sharing, the human is supposed to remain fully immersed into the driving task and be ready at all times to perform the driving task. I've repeatedly warned about the dangers of this co-sharing arrangement and predicted it will produce many untoward results.

Let's focus herein on the true Level 5 self-driving car. Much of the comments apply to the less than Level 5 self-driving cars too, but the fully autonomous AI self-driving car will receive the most attention in this discussion.

Here's the usual steps involved in the AI driving task:
- Sensor data collection and interpretation
- Sensor fusion
- Virtual world model updating
- AI action planning
- Car controls command issuance

Another key aspect of AI self-driving cars is that they will be driving on our roadways in the midst of human driven cars too. There are some pundits of AI self-driving cars that continually refer to a utopian world in which there are only AI self-driving cars on the public roads. Currently there are about 250+ million conventional cars in the United States alone, and those cars are not going to magically disappear or become true Level 5 AI self-driving cars overnight.

Indeed, the use of human driven cars will last for many years, likely many decades, and the advent of AI self-driving cars will occur while there are still human driven cars on the roads. This is a crucial point since this means that the AI of self-driving cars needs to be able to contend with not just other AI self-driving cars, but also contend with human driven cars. It is easy to envision a simplistic and rather unrealistic world in which all AI self-driving cars are politely interacting with each other and being civil about roadway interactions. That's not what is going to be happening for the foreseeable future. AI self-driving cars and human driven cars will need to be able to cope with each other.

Returning to the topic of out-of-control cars and dealing with them as a driver when the car is seemingly out-of-control, let's consider how the AI of an AI self-driving car should be coping with such situations.

We'll start by debunking a popular false myth, namely that true Level 5 AI self-driving cars will never get into car accidents, therefore the claim is that the AI does not need to be able to cope with car crashes.

Wrong!

Well of course AI self-driving cars are going to get into car crashes. It is nonsense to think otherwise.

First, as mentioned earlier, the roadways will have a mixture of human driven cars and AI driven cars. This mixture is going to have car crashes, involving a human driven car that crashes into an AI self-driving car, and likely too occasions whereby an AI self-driving car crashes into a human driven car. In some instances, the AI self-driving car might be the instigator of the car crash, while in other cases it is carried into the car crash as a cascading action of the car crash.

There will also be instances of AI self-driving cars crashing into other AI self-driving cars, as I'll describe in a moment.

Recall that in my story about how I had gotten hit from behind while sitting at a red light, I was in a conventional car, but for pretend sake let's assume that the car was actually a Level 5 AI self-driving car. Would it have been able to avoid getting hit? No. There was no place to escape to and the car that rammed me from behind did so with almost no warning.

The AI might have detected the aspect that the car behind it was suddenly speeding up, and therefore the AI would likely have had a few seconds heads-up that the crash was going to occur. But, given that there was a car immediately ahead of my car, and there were other cars also sitting at the intersection and all around my car, the AI would have been boxed-in or essentially surrounded and would have had no opportunity to escape. The crash would have happened. This is an instance of a human driven car hitting an AI self-driving car.

An AI self-driving car could get hit by another car such as a human driven car and could even get hit by an AI self-driving car.

Suppose the car ahead of me at the intersection was an AI self-driving car and continue assuming that my car was an AI self-driving car. Once the car behind me has hit my car, it would have forced my AI self-driving car to ram into the car ahead, which we're pretending was another AI self-driving car. This is an instance of an AI self-driving car hitting another AI self-driving car.

Some say that an AI self-driving car won't get hit because it will have V2V (vehicle-to-vehicle) electronic communications. This means that one AI self-driving car can electronically communicate with other AI self-driving cars, perhaps doing so to forewarn that the road ahead has debris on it or maybe that the traffic is snarled. Okay, let's assume in my pretend scenario that my AI self-driving car has V2V and the AI self-driving car sitting ahead of me at the intersection has V2V too.

In those few seconds wherein my AI self-driving realizes it is going to get hit, it sends quickly a V2V broadcast, which the AI self-driving car ahead of me receives and decodes. Based on the electronic message, the AI of this car ahead of me has to decide whether it believes what it is being told, which in of itself is a potential question and problem associated with V2V aspects, and if the AI does believe that my car is about to hit it, the next aspect involves figuring out what to do.

The AI self-driving car ahead of me, now forewarned and with presumably a second or two maybe to react, could try to proceed into the intersection to avoid my car hitting it from behind. The AI has to ascertain whether it is worse or not to remain in-place and get hit from behind, or potentially try to gun the engine and rush into the intersection. If the intersection has other traffic in it, the idea of aiming to rush ahead is not so attractive, though likewise staying in place is not attractive either.

This highlights the kind of ethical choices that an AI system is going to need to make when driving an AI self-driving car. It has to decide in this instance the risks of injury, death, damages from waiting to get hit from behind by my AI self-driving car versus the instance of risks of injury, death, damages if it attempts to rush into the intersection. There is also the matter of whether the amount of time involved would actually allow the AI self-driving to rush into the intersection, depending upon the acceleration capability of the AI self-driving car.

I'll give you another example of how an AI self-driving car might hit another AI self-driving car. Suppose there are two AI self-driving cars are going down a street (hey, this sounds like an AI self-driving car joke of some kind, like two people going into a bar!). They are following each other at the proper distance, based on their speeds and car lengths, and is supposed to be how humans are to drive a car, though I'd wager few humans allow sufficient distances between their cars when driving.

A dog darts from seemingly nowhere and into the street. In this case, there was no possibility of detecting the dog prior to its entering into the street. The AI self-driving car that's ahead of the other AI self-driving car has insufficient distance to come to a stop and avoid hitting the dog. The choices for the AI are to either try to stop and yet know it will ram into the dog, or try to swerve to avoid the dog, but let's assume there are parked cars and other cars coming down the street too.

This means that the AI will need to decide whether to hit and likely kill the dog or take a chance and swerve into the oncoming lane of traffic and possibly get hit head-on or ram itself into a parked car to try and avoid the dog.

What should the AI do?

The AI is between the proverbial rock and a hard place. There aren't any "good" choices to be made here. Which is the least of the worst options is more akin to this problem. Suppose the AI opts to ram into a parked car, figuring that the parked car has no humans in it and thus no humans will be put at risk, and it is only property damage that will result. This saves the dog, prevents potentially hitting an oncoming car, and perhaps seems to be the least-of-the-worst choices.

The AI quickly sends out a V2V to forewarn that it is going to ram into a parked car. The AI self-driving car coming up behind is given a somewhat sudden heads-up that this action is going to occur. Can the AI self-driving car stop in time and avoid hitting the AI self-driving car that is going to ram into the parked car? Maybe yes, maybe not. We also don't know if the ramming into the parked car will cause the AI self-driving car to perhaps bounce back into the street and maybe make the situation from the perspective of the upcoming AI self-driving car even worse.

The point of these scenarios is that there will absolutely be car crashes involving AI self-driving cars. I want to make sure that we all agree with that possibility. Some might argue that we'll have less car crashes due to the advent of AI self-driving cars, and for that I'd be willing to say it is hopefully the case that we'll have less, but in no manner at all will we have zero instances of car crashes involving AI self-driving cars.

In terms of AI self-driving cars and getting involved into car crashes, most of the auto makers and tech firms are focused on avoiding car crashes and not particularly considering what the AI should do once a car crash is imminent or underway.

This is troubling.

If the AI is not intentionally established to have special processes or procedures for dealing with a car accident once underway, it means that the AI self-driving car is essentially going to become out-of-control.

The AI developers are assuming that the AI will be able to handle the self-driving car as if the AI self-driving car is just nonchalantly driving along, but once the car accident starts, all such bets are off. The AI self-driving car is going to be likely pushed, shoved, and otherwise taken out of the "comfort zone" in which one assumes the self-driving car is operating most of the time. Assumptions about being able to brake, accelerate, and steer are no longer going to be valid due to the extenuating circumstances involving what is about to happen to the self-driving car.

Some auto makers and tech firms aren't working on this at all, or they are working on it but put it on the backburner as a so-called edge problem. Their logic to put this on the backburner is that they assume the AI self-driving car is highly unlikely to get into a car accident, thus, why worry about it now. If it is going to only happen once in a blue moon, deal with it later on.

Part of the grave concern with this kind of thinking is that it means that when an AI self-driving car does get into a car accident, it will likely do little to try and minimize the impacts and be unable or ill-equipped to find ways to either escape or at least try to "improve" upon a bad situation.

I've predicted many times over that when AI self-driving cars get into car crashes, society is going to become hyper-focused on why and how it happened, and the entire future of AI self-driving cars is going to be based on these instances. It becomes the classic "bad apple" that spoils the entire barrel. I know many AI developers are frustrated that this can occur and feel that it is unfair of society and the media to react in such a manner, but, hey, that's the way the cookie crumbles.

Generally, the public and the media are not especially forgiving about AI self-driving cars getting involved in car accidents.

Tesla's Elon Musk has bitterly complained that society over-hypes these instances and should try to balance those instances against the thousands of car accidents with conventional cars, but he's barking up a rough tree to think that society will be willing to view AI self-driving cars in that kind of context.

Auto makers and tech firms need to be doing as much as they can to cope with not only avoiding car crashes but also being able to have the AI enter into a kind of "crash mode" when a car accident is either imminent or underway.

I would likely anticipate that if the auto makers and tech firms don't have such a provision in their AI, besides the aspect that it means the AI will be somewhat acting in a willy-nilly manner during a car accident, I would predict that the auto makers and tech firms are going to be faced with some hefty legal bills and potential product liability issues. Lawyers for those humans that are immersed in a car accident are going to ask tough questions about what the AI did, why it did so, etc.

As suggested earlier, let's put a stopwatch into the car accident aspects and assume that at the initial point of impact we start the clocking ticking. This is almost as though we are able to slow down time and do a slow-motion analysis of a car accident.

In a manner of speaking, we might look at this from the perspective of "speeding up" rather than slowing down. A human might not be able to give much mental concentration to a car accident once the accident begins to unfold. The time allotted is very short, perhaps fractions of a second or just a few split seconds. On the other hand, the AI might be running on some very fast computer processors and so it could potentially do a lot of computational processing in that rather short amount of time.

There are those that would argue too that the AI won't go into shock and so it will keep its head about it, while a human is likely to not keep their presence of mind. In my car accident, I still don't know what exactly happened from the moment of impact until I was suddenly aware that I was seated in my car and something untoward had just occurred. Whether I was in shock or maybe blacked out momentarily, we presumably don't need to worry about the AI suffering that same fate.

I would though wish to put a caveat on this idea that the AI won't suffer from the shock aspects. Those that make such a claim are leaving out the important element that the AI is running on computer processors that are on-board the self-driving car. When the self-driving car is getting rammed, there is a high chance that those processors are going to suffer too. The physics of the situation can mess with the electronics. The physical crushing actions and blows to the car are likely to mess with the electronics of the computer processors and computer memory on-board the self-driving car.

In a manner of speaking, you could assert that there is a chance that the AI will go into "shock" or maybe we call it "artificial shock," involving damage being done to the AI systems and its on-board computers. This could alter what the AI is able to do during the crash itself. What kind of fail-safe capabilities does the AI have?

Maybe the AI is not able to do anything once the crash gets underway and has become completely inoperative.

Maybe the AI is messed up and does not realize that it has become messed up, and yet still tries to drive the car, doing so in a manner that actually makes the situation worse!

Overall, the special "crash mode" of the AI needs to be able to discern what it can and cannot do, what its own status is in terms of working properly, and have a number of contingencies ready to go.

There is no doubting that the "crash mode" becomes a highly complex problem. The self-driving car is likely becoming less drivable as the car crash clock ticks, starting at point in time t=0. At some time, we'll say is t+1, perhaps the brakes are no longer functioning. At some time, t+2, it could be that the car is now in a slide as a result of the ramming and the wheels are unable to gain traction to redirect the direction of the self-driving car. And so on.

I had earlier mentioned that I wasn't sure in my car accident as to the capability of my limbs, such as whether I still had any ability to keep my arms and hands on the steering wheel or have my foot on the brake pedal. The AI is going to have similar "driving controls" issues to cope with. Though the AI doesn't have arms or legs, it does have electronic systems and various means to undertake the driving controls of the self-driving car. Are those driving controls still available to the AI or might they have been damaged or cut as a result of the underway car crash as it evolves in those split seconds?

In essence, you have these aspects:

- AI system as "mindset" for driving the car

- Sensors of the self-driving car that the AI needs to sense what's happening

- Car controls for the AI to use to drive or control the self-driving car

The AI system itself might be degraded or faulty during the car crash and must have a provision to ascertain its own status and reliability.

This then would be used to try and decide what actions the AI ought to be taking, and also avoid taking actions that the AI ought to not be taking.

The sensors such as the cameras, the LIDAR, the radar, and the ultrasonic can become degraded or faulty during the car crash. This means that whatever the sensor fusion is reporting might be false or incomplete. This means that the updating of the virtual world model might be false or faulty. The AI action planner needs to try and ascertain what about the sensors and virtual world model seem to make sense and what aspects might now be suspect.

The car controls might no longer be accessible by the AI, due to the car crash aspects as they unfold. Or, maybe the AI can issue car controls commands, but the controls themselves are nonresponsive, or the car controls attempt to carry out the order, but the physics of the car and the evolving situation preclude the car from physically being able to carry out the instructions.

One aspect that I've not brought up herein involves the AI having to decide what to do about any human passengers that are in the AI self-driving car. This is quite important and must be taken into consideration.

Here's what I mean.

For the AI to consider what action to take during the car crash, there is the matter of how the humans within the AI self-driving car are going to be impacted too. Which is better or worse for the passengers, having the AI attempt to accelerate out of the full impact or instead maybe letting the impact happen but steer the car so that the impact happens on one side of the car versus the side that the humans are sitting in?

The crux is that the number of human passengers, where they are seated, possibly their size and age (adult versus child), could all play into how to "best" respond to the car crash as it is underway. This takes us again into an ethics laden situation. If the AI can find a means to more likely save let's say an adult in the self-driving car versus the child, should it take such action, or should it attempt to save the child more so than the adult?

I know that you might be saying that the AI should seek to save all humans inside of the AI self-driving car. Sorry, that's too easy an answer. There is a myriad of options that the AI might be able to consider. Each of those options will involve uncertainties. We also need to consider the humans outside of the AI self-driving car, such as there might be pedestrians standing nearby that are at risk, and humans in the other nearby cars that are cascading into the car crash.

The AI has quite an arduous problem to solve during a car crash. That's partially why it is being avoided by some AI developers, it is a really tough nut to crack. I don't think though that this means that we should just shrug it off and wave our hands in the air. Without any kind of crash mode capability, the AI is going to be potentially useless and merely add fuel to the fire of the self-driving car becoming a kind of unguided missile.

When I say this, there are some that try to retort that the AI might have a crash mode and try to deal with a car crash as it evolves, and yet ultimately be unable to do anything of substance anyway. It might be that the car controls are unavailable or nonfunctioning. It might be that the choices of what to do are so rotten that doing nothing is a better choice. Etc.

Yes, it is true that the AI might end-up not being able to aid the lessening of the car crash repercussions. Does this mean though that the AI should not even try to do so? Are you willing to toss away the chance that the AI might be able to assist? I don't believe that's prudent and nor what we might hope a true AI self-driving car will do.

Each situation will have its own particulars that dictate what becomes feasible during the crash. Was there any in-advance indication of what was about to occur? Was any preparation possible prior to the actual crash? Once the crash began, what possibilities existed of still being able to exert control over the self-driving car? Throughout the car crash, what could be done and what was done?

There's also the post-crash aspects too. If the AI self-driving is still in some functionable capability, the AI should be trying to ascertain what to do. Is the car still drivable by the AI such that the AI can pull the self-driving car off to the side of the road, and avoid possibly getting hit therefore by other traffic that might be soon coming upon the accident scene?

The AI must be continually monitoring the car controls status to try and discern what is usable and what is not:

- No steering, limited steering, steering is stuck

- No accelerator, limited accelerator, accelerator stuck

- No brakes, limited brakes, brakes stuck

Here's a bit of twist that might catch your interest.

Some say that we should be using Machine Learning (ML) or Deep Learning (DL) to cope with and aid the crafting of the special "crash mode" of the AI for a self-driving car.

The notion is that the use of deep or large-scale artificial neural networks might allow the AI to identify patterns in what to do during car crashes. By examining perhaps hundreds or thousands of car crashes, in the same way that the ML or DL studies pictures of street signs to identify what street signs consist of, maybe the AI could become versed in handling car crashes.

This seems sensible. One question for you, where are we going to get all of this car crash data that will be needed to do the ML or DL training? Right now, the AI self-driving cars and auto makers and tech firms are doing everything they can to avoid car crashes. There isn't a vast trove of car crash data available to do this kind of pattern matching and training with.

Sure, there are tons of car crashes daily that are occurring with conventional cars. This though does not encompass the kind of car crash data that we need to have collected. For today's car crashes, at best there is info about what happened before a crash and what the end result was. Whatever happened in-between is not particularly data captured and nor analyzed.

Unfortunately, there is not a handy treasure trove of car crash data that includes what took place during the crash itself. The closest that we can come would be to use simulations. The simulations though need to be based on the reality of what happens during car crashes. This might seem obvious, but I point this out because it is "easy" to make a simulation based on aspects that have little to do with what really happens in the real-world. Training via ML or DL via simulations that aren't realistic is not likely to be overly helpful, though it at least provides a potential step forward.

Conclusion

We need to have the AI of a self-driving car be able to deal with car crashes. This includes not just the pre-crash aspects and the post-crash aspects, which is usually where the attention by the AI developers is aimed. There must be a "crash mode" that is able to cope with the unwinding or evolving elements that happen during a car crash.

The crash mode could be a kind of last-resort core portion that does what it can to try and keep aware of the moment-to-moment situation and exert any car control that it can, doing so in hopes of minimizing injury, death, or damages. Similar to humans, in a manner of speaking, the AI can suffer from a type of "artificial shock" that means it will become degraded in being able to figure out what is taking place and what can be done about the emerging situation.

The complexities during a crash are enormous. What on the self-driving car is still working and usable? What is the status of the humans on-board? What is the situation outside of the self-driving car? How can all of these variables be coalesced into a sensible plan of action and carried out by the AI? The odds are that whatever the AI derives, the plan itself will need to be instantly re-planned, based on the aspect that the situation is rapidly changing.

Other than demolition derby drivers, I'd suggest that most drivers are unable to remain steady and have the presence of mind during a car accident to do much to mitigate the consequences. The AI has a chance to be that demolition derby driver, though let's subtract the part about wanting to purposely hit other cars as is the goal of a derby.

The AI potentially has fast-enough processing speed to try and find ways to cope with the car crash while it is occurring and take rudimentary actions related to the self-driving car. For the sake of AI self-driving cars, and for the sake of human lives, let's put some keen focus on having "crash mode" savvy AI.

CHAPTER 5
SOUNDING OUT CAR NOISES
AND
AI SELF-DRIVING CARS

CHAPTER 5

SOUNDING OUT

CAR NOISES

AND

AI SELF-DRIVING CARS

The sounds of silence. You might have thought that I was referring to the famous song by Simon and Garfunkel, but I am actually referring to the moments in which silence is golden. In particular, I'm referring to cars that are "silent" in that they aren't making any rattling, grinding, clanging, or banging sounds as you happen to be riding in them.

Usually, any such ear catching sounds are bound to mean that there is something wrong with the car and you are likely at risk while riding in the vehicle.

At any moment, the engine might seize up, the axle might crack and fail, or any number of maladies might emerge. The sounds emanating from the car can be a handy sign that something is amiss and often precedes the whole-hog failure of a part or element of the car. Of course, sometimes the disturbing noise coincides with the actual failure event itself, in which case, the car problem is likely more apparent than the noise that you might have heard (the car sharply swerving, or the engine halting tends to draw more attention than the noise itself).

In college, I knew an amateur car mechanic that delighted in telling me what each car noise might mean in terms of the potential problem with a car. He was a walking and talking encyclopedia of car sounds and noises. He had an audible superpower worthy of being featured in a Marvel movie or comic book series. You could ask him what it means to hear a clanking, followed by a clicking, followed again by more clanking. He could tell you that it was likely you had a problem with your suspension, or the brakes, or the exhaust system, or whatever part of the car that he figured made those kinds of noises.

There's a popular radio and TV commercial airing recently that has people making seemingly silly noises with their mouth and noses, attempting to replicate the sounds they heard their car making. A savvy car specialist that has "heard it all" watches them make these noises and calmly tells them what is most likely wrong with their cars. I'd bet that you at one time or another have tried to describe an issue of your car by telling others that the car was making a weird or unusual noise, and you valiantly tried to make the sound by vocalizing it. We all do so.

As an aside, my writing down these sounds herein and using words such as bam, bang, clang, are considered examples of onomatopoeia. When you say that a cow goes moo or a sheep goes baa-baa, you are making use of an onomatopoeicword. These are words that attempt to reflect phonetically the sound of something and somewhat resemble or suggest the actual sound that we hear. If you didn't already know that word, figured you'd want to add it to your vocabulary.

A car does not necessarily need to make any special sounds or noises before something goes awry. I mention this aspect because you can have a part or element that decides to quit on you and can do so without having to make an adverse and noticeable sound. I had a timing belt that just abruptly snapped on my car.

There usually is a warning, often heard as a slipping sound of the belt not being able to remain clinging in place. You've undoubtedly heard a slipping belt sound many times. In this somewhat rare instance, my car belt opted to completely snap in two and did so without being polite enough to warn me beforehand.

Speaking of being polite, in a manner of speaking, the untoward sounds and noises that a car makes is actually a handy and helpful act for us humans. Assuming that the sound or noise occurs before a bad turn of events occurs, the car is presumably trying to give you a heads-up to be on the watch. People that choose to ignore these warning sounds are doing so at their own peril.

I had a friend that bitterly complained that his car kept making numerous horrible noises. Darn it, he proclaimed, he wished the darn-blasted car would stop making all those irritating and excruciating sounds. I would ask him whether he thought that the car should magically self-repair itself and thus extinguish making these noises?

I would further point out that the noises are a welcome reminder that maybe he ought to have someone look at his car and figure out what is wrong with it. Perhaps now might be timely to make needed repairs or perform car maintenance that he had most likely forsaken to do. Imagine if he opted to drive on a long trip in a barren place, let's say driving through a desert, and the car falls apart, which he could have anticipated beforehand by the noises the car was making and hopefully have not gotten stuck in the middle of nowhere.

For me, I'm appreciative when a car makes those seemingly unwelcome sounds or noises.

How lucky that the car has kindly chosen to let me know something is amiss. If you had a pet dog or cat, and the pet started to make untoward sounds, you'd likely be worried that something was amiss. You'd look closely at the dog or cat, trying to figure out what is wrong. Assuming you could not readily discern the problem, the odds are that you'd take your pet to see a veterinarian.

I suppose you might first tell your friends the sounds your pet was making, in hopes they might know what the problem is, doing so before having to go to the trouble to visit a veterinarian.

We tend to do the same thing with our cars. There's an untoward sound or noise. You might tell a friend about it, asking them if they've ever heard such a noise. The friend might say they had the same sound when the car needed a tune-up, and so you opt to take your car into a tune-up shop. Or, your friends might say they've never heard such a sound in a car before. You then need to decide whether to take the car to a repair or maintenance facility.

Admittedly, none of us want to hassle taking our car in. You need to go out of your way to drive to such a place. You need to wait for a trained mechanic or similar to take a look at your car. You need to have them diagnose what it might mean. Then, you fearfully wait to hear how much it will cost to repair it and dread the length of time needed for your car to be in the shop and unavailable to you. The whole process is daunting and undesirable, for sure.

Your mind considers other possibilities. Maybe the sound isn't so bad. It could be a sound that will go away on its own. If you ignore it, somehow the car will realize that you aren't giving in to the irritating sound. It's like a child that keeps pestering you to take them to the ice cream parlor. Let the kid ask a bunch of times, ignore the requests, and in the end perhaps the child will give up asking about it. Could car sounds be that way too, you wonder?

The thing is that sometimes a car sound does indeed go away. This emboldens us to consider ignoring such sounds or otherwise discounting them. I knew it, you might say to yourself, I successfully ignored that sound for two weeks and now it has stopped making the irksome noise. Thank goodness you didn't take the car into a mechanic. All they would have done was charge you a fee to tell you that the noise was nonsense and you can merely continue to drive the car as usual.

This idea that the sound has disappeared and there is no concern that the sound occurred to begin with, well, that can also be a kind of lazy person's trap.

It could be that the thing that is going wrong has gotten even worse. In the worsened state, the noise might no longer be generated. I know that seems counter-intuitive, namely that if the problem is getting worse then the noise certainly should be getting worse, but not everything works that way. You can have a problem that in fact is worsening and yet the sound either goes away, or it becomes some other kind of sound, perhaps a sound less obvious or less threatening.

The other perturbing aspect is that suppose you do opt to take your car into a mechanic, and yet the sound perchance no longer is being emitted. The car mechanic might look at you as though you are crazy. I swear on my solemn oath, you tell the mechanic, it was making this clang-clang sound. The mechanic starts the car, listens carefully, listens patiently, but no such sound occurs. Shrugging their shoulders, the mechanic might say come back once it actually is making the sound and they will take another look.

Equally frustrating involves the mechanic not only unable to hear the sound, and an assertion that without the sound they cannot tell you what might be wrong, but they then offer they must do a complete diagnosis of your car. Big bucks! This is likely to have you roll your eyes in despair and disgust.

Rather than having the mechanic focus on the specific aspect that is presumably wrong with the car, the mechanic is going to charge you to go on a fishing expedition. You know in your bones that the mechanic is going to find 20 things wrong with your car, even though that's not what you came into the mechanic for. You went from one little itty bitty sound to instead having to get your entire car nearly overhauled.

On the topic of trying to use the car's sounds for diagnosis purposes, it at times makes sense that the mechanic might not hear the noises that you heard. Suppose the sound only arises when the car is actually in-motion. If you take your car to the repair shop and while it is parked you turn on the car, this might not be a sufficient replication of the circumstances under which the sound is generated. There is the strong possibility that the noise only arises when the car is in actual motion.

I knew one person that drove their car around and within the parking lot of the repair shop and still could not get the noise to appear. This is another viable possibility since the noise might only arise when the car is in faster motion, perhaps while going 65 miles per hour on the freeway. Going a few measly miles per hour in a parking lot at a snail's pace could be insufficient to get the sound to announce itself.

Another factor can involve whether the car is heated-up. Sometimes a noise might occur only when the engine is cold and upon first starting the car. In other cases, the noise only arises after the car has been going for a solid 30 minutes or more and the engine and the car components are heated-up. This undermines those occasions whereby you take your car to the repair shop, let it sit there, parked and the engine is no longer going, and they then turn it on and try to hear the sound that you experienced earlier.

The number of variants is rather daunting. Maybe the sound only occurs while shifting gears. Perhaps the sound only happens when the car is taking a sharp turn. The noise might arise when going uphill, or only when going downhill. This highlights that where the car is being driven can make a difference in stoking the noise, along with how the car is being driven.

A family member used to ride her brakes all of the time. At one point, she complained that whenever she put her foot on the brakes, there was a loud shrieking sound. I took the car for a short drive to see if I could hear the sound. Upon doing so, I was unable to replicate the noise. I then tried to put myself into her mindset, or you might say into her shoes, and I decided to start riding the brakes continuously. I would normally only use the brakes as needed and when needed. In any case, sure enough, after a few minutes of continually riding the brakes, the shrieking sound arose.

When I got back after doing the test drive, I was actually temped to say that the shrieking sound was a child's squeaky toy that was jammed under the brake pedal. Ha! Actually, though I make light of the situation, there are car mechanics that I've spoken with that claim they have had similar kinds of circumstances. They popped up the hood and found a kid's toy that somehow got stuck into part of the car. One joked that after a complaint of banging sounds coming from the trunk area, the mechanic "discovered" that it was Jimmy Hoffa, trying to knock-knock and get out of the trunk (I told the mechanic that Jimmy Hoffa jokes are wearing thin as the Gen Z isn't quite in tune with such humor).

A key aspect about car sounds is that you usually need to know when they arose. Where was the person driving the car? Type of road surfaces can make a difference, elevation cam make a difference, and other roadway and infrastructure factors come to play. How were they driving, such as with a lead foot or a light touch? At one point of a driving journey did the sound begin, at the start or midway or toward the end?

Yet another factor is whether the sound is a one-time instance, or whether it is intermittent or periodic. One-time only sounds can be especially difficult to figure out. With the intermittent or periodic sounds, you usually have a greater chance of hearing it and also speculating as to what might be causing it.

There is the sound that is subtle and barely audible, while there are the noises or sounds that are unmistakable and boldly proclaimed. A sound might begin with barely being heard and gradually become an overwhelming grinding or pinging noise. On the other hand, the sound might begin with a huge and shocking bang, and then become a low hum that you are unsure whether it is making any sound or not.

I've also not yet mentioned that the sound or noise might change over time and get intertwined with other sounds too. It could be that the first sound you hear is a hissing. The hiss seems to disappear. You then hear a rumbling noise. The rumbling noise dissipates. Now you hear an ugly popping sound. What is going on? Is your car possessed by evil spirits?

You continue driving and are keeping your fingers crossed that these noises don't mean that your car is about to fall apart while on the road. You begin to hear the hissing sound again. Oh no, it has returned. This time though you hear the hiss and then you begin to also hear the rumbling noise. Yikes! Then, the popping sound joins into the cacophony. You are having your own car musical band that has decided to play all the instruments at once. It's a scary rendition.

Here's another scenario. I was in someone else's car and thought I heard a rattling sound. The other person was driving, and we were zooming along on the German autobahn. I looked furtively at the driver and was trying to see whether she had heard the sound. She seemed not to have heard it. The radio was on and there was music playing through the impressive speakers of the car.

I realized that the music was potentially masking or overpowering the rattling sound that I had heard. I reached over and dialed down the volume of the radio. Sure enough, the driver then heard the sound. I guess my ears were a bit more tuned to hearing car sounds. Or, perhaps the music that was playing on the radio wasn't to my liking and I wasn't listening intently to it.

The point being that there might be other sounds or noises occurring inside the car and might have nothing to do with car-specific sounds or noises. This can make it hard to differentiate the car-specific sounds from the rest of the sounds occurring in the car. My ears were able to differentiate the music from the rattling sound. Not everyone would necessarily be able to separate out such sounds. Realizing this, I had purposely turned down the volume so that the driver could also hear the sound.

You might be thinking that these various car sounds and noises that relate to something untoward about the car are all ad hoc and have no pattern to them. Not so!

As mentioned, car mechanics can often make a pretty good guess about what might be wrong with your car via hearing the sound that it is making.

The car mechanic doesn't necessarily need to hear the actual sound and can use your description of the sound to make a guess about what is wrong. Your description of the sound might be in words only (possibly using onomatopoeic words), or you might try to replicate the sound by making your own gurgling and popping noises.

Today, there are several online databases of car sounds and noises, along with indicating what the noise or sound might suggest about any problems of your car. You can go to the database and listen to the sounds, trying to see if any match to the sound you heard in your car. You can also try recording the sound that occurs in your car and try to get it to match to the database, doing a calculation-type of matching using a sound conversion algorithm.

I don't want to overstate the use of such online databases. Your particular brand and model of car might make a difference in the kind of sound emitted from your car and not match well to what's in the database. The sounds in the databases are at times somewhat generic, or in other cases are specific to particular car brands and models. I'd suggest that though these repositories are handy, but you are still going to ultimately need an actual car mechanic to take a look and a listen to your car.

I'd also say that those of you that might decide to record a sound and then when you get home try to look it up, keep in mind that this might be a chancy act of delay. Suppose the sound is one that is serious enough that something bad is going to happen to your car right away. You might want to get that car to a repair shop, rather than waiting to try and figure out what the problem is.

For those of you that are versed enough to be your own car mechanic, I don't want you to feel that I'm pushing everyone to go to a car mechanic. If you have the knowledge and experience to care for your car, that's great! I am merely attempting to emphasize that sometimes people don't take their car noises seriously and therefore get themselves into worse trouble. In whatever manner you react to your car sounds, make sure to give them their due, taking action as needed.

What does this have to do with AI self-driving cars?

At the Cybernetic AI Self-Driving Car Institute, we are developing AI software for self-driving cars. Detecting car sounds and noises is a helpful and some might say essential added element that the AI ought to be providing in a self-driving car.

Allow me to elaborate.

I'd like to first clarify and introduce the notion that there are varying levels of AI self-driving cars. The topmost level is considered Level 5. A Level 5 self-driving car is one that is being driven by the AI and there is no human driver involved. For the design of Level 5 self-driving cars, the auto makers are even removing the gas pedal, brake pedal, and steering wheel, since those are contraptions used by human drivers. The Level 5 self-driving car is not being driven by a human and nor is there an expectation that a human driver will be present in the self-driving car. It's all on the shoulders of the AI to drive the car.

For self-driving cars less than a Level 5, there must be a human driver present in the car. The human driver is currently considered the responsible party for the acts of the car. The AI and the human driver are co-sharing the driving task. In spite of this co-sharing, the human is supposed to remain fully immersed into the driving task and be ready at all times to perform the driving task. I've repeatedly warned about the dangers of this co-sharing arrangement and predicted it will produce many untoward results.

Let's focus herein on the true Level 5 self-driving car. Much of the comments apply to the less than Level 5 self-driving cars too, but the fully autonomous AI self-driving car will receive the most attention in this discussion.

Here's the usual steps involved in the AI driving task:

- Sensor data collection and interpretation

- Sensor fusion

- Virtual world model updating

- AI action planning

- Car controls command issuance

Another key aspect of AI self-driving cars is that they will be driving on our roadways in the midst of human driven cars too. There are some pundits of AI self-driving cars that continually refer to a utopian world in which there are only AI self-driving cars on the public roads. Currently there are about 250+ million conventional cars in the United States alone, and those cars are not going to magically disappear or become true Level 5 AI self-driving cars overnight.

Indeed, the use of human driven cars will last for many years, likely many decades, and the advent of AI self-driving cars will occur while there are still human driven cars on the roads. This is a crucial point since this means that the AI of self-driving cars needs to be able to contend with not just other AI self-driving cars, but also contend with human driven cars. It is easy to envision a simplistic and rather unrealistic world in which all AI self-driving cars are politely interacting with each other and being civil about roadway interactions. That's not what is going to be happening for the foreseeable future. AI self-driving cars and human driven cars will need to be able to cope with each other. Period.

Returning to the topic of car sounds and noises, let's consider how this might be handled by AI self-driving cars.

First, true Level 5 AI self-driving cars will be equipped with internal microphones for the primary purpose of interacting with human passengers.

Humans inside an AI self-driving car will most certainly need to have an ongoing dialogue with the AI system, using an AI-equipped Natural Language Processing (NLP) capability, so that the human can indicate where they want to go. In addition, the human and the AI will likely have discussions about intermediary potential destinations and cover other topics such as whether the ride should be scenic or focused on getting to the desired destination and similar matters.

With those microphones already inside an AI self-driving car, the potential for also using that equipment as listening devices to detect car sounds and noises is readily heightened. I realize you might assume that the microphones would absolutely be used to listen for car noises, but I'll offer some caveats about why that might not be quite so certain.

One issue that has yet to be resolved involves the privacy elements of passengers inside true Level 5 AI self-driving cars.

While you are a passenger in an AI self-driving car, should the microphones be activated and possibly recording your every word? For some, this is a significant potential intrusion into their privacy. Though some auto makers and tech firms might say they won't keep the recorded conversations, this is not assured and there could be reasons that the auto maker or tech firm might feel compelled to give over such recordings (due to law enforcement or court requests, etc.).

If you believe the existing makers of various speech-oriented devices such as Alexa and Siri, it is claimed that until those systems hear the prearranged designated word, such as the name of the service, there is nothing being recorded. Instead, the NLP is supposedly scanning streaming audio and looking only for the activation word. Once the activation word is heard, the NLP then starts processing the conversation and may or might not be keeping a recording of the audio.

Let's then consider what might occur while you are inside an AI self-driving car. If the AI is only listening for the magical keyword for activation, this implies it is not activated per se until it hears the keyword, and therefore it is not actively listening for car sounds or noises. In that case, the only time at which the AI has an opportunity to listen for car sounds and noises would be once the human passenger has uttered the activation word.

You might at first say that waiting until the passenger says the activation word seems fine. The problem of course is that if the sound occurs prior to the passenger saying the activation word, the AI won't know or won't have recorded the sound. This could mean that a crucial sound or noise was not detected. It could also be that once the passenger has uttered the activation word, perhaps the sound does not repeat itself. This is nearly akin to going to see your car mechanic and claiming you heard a sound, but the car mechanic has no means to hear it themselves.

This gap in hearing such sounds or noises is a trade-off of the potential privacy intrusion.

One also has to consider whether the passenger will even have the presence of mind to activate the AI if there is a noise or sound heard. It could be that the passenger fails to realize that they could have the AI help in trying to determine what the sound entails. Plus, if a child is in the self-driving car and there is no adult present, it would seem less likely that the child would realize it might be prudent to activate the AI in the matter.

You might suggest that the AI would be activated when a human utters a prearranged keyword, plus it would activate automatically whenever a car sound or noise is detected. In that case, the AI NLP is searching for not just a particular keyword. It is also searching for various kinds of sounds. Once one of those sounds or noises is detected, the AI would potentially start to more actively listen, and might alert the human passenger accordingly.

The downside with this approach is that there is a chance that other sounds or noises that are not especially related to the car itself might inadvertently cause this kind of activation.

You can imagine the potential irritation to a passenger if they are playing some game or music inside the self-driving car and the AI keeps falsely alerting that it believes a car sound or noise has occurred. The potential for false positives might be so much that passengers would not want the AI to be activating when it hears such sounds.

Another aspect to be considered is whether the "normal" microphones used to interact with the passengers will be sufficient for purposes of identifying and "hearing" the car sounds and noises that might occur.

If the microphones are positioned in a manner to pick-up the human voice, they might not be well-positioned for picking up car sounds or noises, which would usually emanate from below the flooring of the car. This might necessitate adding additional microphones into the self-driving car, which also adds cost, weight, and potentially impacts the interior design and space available. It might even make sense to have specialized microphones that aren't for conversing with humans and instead installed solely for detecting the car sounds and noises.

This does bring up another facet of the car sounds and noises. Suppose a human passenger hears a car sound or noise, and they wonder what it might mean. It is conceivable the human passenger might ask the AI about the sound or noise. Did you hear that, the human asks the AI. What was that sound, the humans asks the AI.

I know that some AI developers cringe at having to add such aspects to the NLP dialogue capabilities of the AI system. For most AI developers that are currently working on self-driving cars, they are already overwhelmed with other matters that they consider more important. To them, the detection of car sounds is a far cry from anything core to a self-driving car. They would say that this is all an "edge" problem, meaning something that is at the far edge or corner of what really needs to be done, and so can be set aside until a much later time to consider it.

In any case, it certainly seems likely that a human passenger would ask the AI about the car sounds or noises.

If you were in a ridesharing car or a cab driven by a human, and you heard a seemingly disturbing sound coming from the car, I would bet that you'd ask the human driver about it. You'd want to validate that they heard the sound too. You'd hope that the driver might know what the sound presages. You would want the driver to be on alert about the driving of the car, based on qualms about hearing untoward sounds or noises emanating from the car.

Human passengers in an AI self-driving car are going to react in the same manner, beseeching the AI to verify having heard the sound, along with aiming to get some explanation from the AI about it. Most importantly, the human passenger wants the AI to be watchful of the self-driving car since the sounds might foretell something bad about to happen. Will the AI be able to handle the driving safely if the sound is a precursor to a physical breakdown of some part of the car?

This is where the AI and NLP aspects get quite tricky. Suppose the AI says that there is a 30% chance that the knocking sound means that a rod in the engine is about to fail. Yikes, the passenger screams! Get me out of this self-driving car, now! This estimation of the probability might falsely give the impression to the human that the whole car is about to fall apart. It could cause a needless panic.

This raises the important question about how the AI should interact with humans about the sounds or noises that were heard. Do you want an AI that offers soothing words? Do you want an AI that tells it like it is, though the indication might be perceived as brash or harsh? A human driver would likely alter their response to a human passenger depending upon a multitude of factors, such as their own perceived seriousness about the noise, and the nature of the passenger and how they might cope with such a discussion.

We also need to consider that a human passenger might get startled at a sound or noise that has nothing to do with the car at all. Suppose the self-driving car happens to drive past a construction site and there is an explosive sound that comes from the construction taking place there. The human hears the loud bang and thinks it came from the self-driving car. The human asks the AI what the sound was.

If the AI did not hear the sound, perhaps being muffled by the car windows being closed, it might say that it did not hear the sound. This could spark the person toward further panic because they might then believe that the AI is not paying attention or has failed to detect something that might be very vital to the self-driving car safety.

One potential advantage of having the AI detecting for car sounds and noises would be that it might be able to do an extensive analysis on the car sound. A human driver of a ridesharing service might not know much about cars. For them, any sounds are just sounds, and they might not have a clue as to what a particular ping or pop signifies. The AI could look-up the sounds in a database and potentially have a better means of discerning what the sound portends.

We could carry this capability to a more advanced level for the AI.

Suppose the AI system had a knowledge-based component that could do an in-depth diagnosis to a level similar to a car mechanic hearing a noise. This more advanced capability could aid the self-driving car in diagnosing the potential problem and would also aid the ongoing driving of the self-driving car by the AI.

If the sound occurs whenever the AI takes a sharp left turn, the AI action planning portion might opt to be especially careful making left turns. This could avoid for the moment further harming whatever mechanical issue has occurred.

Via OTA (Over-the-Air) electronic communications, which the AI usually uses to pump data up to the cloud of the auto maker or tech firm, and gets patches and updates pushed down to the on-board AI system, the AI could share the sounds or noises into the cloud. This might be handy as there might be other similar noises or sounds that have been heard in other AI self-driving cars of this particular fleet.

If the AI self-driving car is part of a ridesharing service, the AI might then confer with some master scheduling system and indicate that the self-driving car needs to get over to a repair shop. The self-driving car might finish up the delivery of the human passenger and then route itself over to the maintenance facility. The cloud would meanwhile realize that this AI self-driving car is temporarily out of service.

In terms of the types of actions that the AI might take, doing so after detecting and diagnosing a car sound or noise, these are potential AI planning action steps:

- Stop use of the self-driving car "immediately" and pull over safely

- Stop use of the self-driving car as soon as practical and seek to get to a repair shop

- Adjust the driving of the self-driving car based on the potential issue

- Continue normal use of the self-driving car and note to have the matter checked

- Consider the sound or noise irrelevant and take no other action due to it

- Etc.

Another potential recourse would be for the AI self-driving car to institute an electronic dialogue with other nearby AI self-driving cars. Using V2V (vehicle-to-vehicle) electronic communications, the AI self-driving car that has detected an untoward sound might request that other nearby AI self-driving cars take a look at the AI self-driving car to see if they detect anything untoward. For example, if the tailpipe is dragging on the street, an AI self-driving car that is behind this AI self-driving car could detect the dragging tailpipe via the use of its cameras.

The V2V dialogue might also be used to warn other nearby AI self-driving cars that the AI self-driving car initiating the dialogue might soon be exhibiting driving issues. Perhaps the self-driving car is going to start weaving, due to a mechanical breakdown, and the AI will be doing whatever it can to minimize the weaving. Meanwhile, other nearby AI self-driving cars have intentionally given a wider berth for the weaving AI self-driving car, doing so as a result of being forewarned about a potential car problem.

In addition, the use of V2I (vehicle-to-infrastructure) electronic communication might be useful. The AI self-driving car that has encountered untoward sounds might warn the roadway infrastructure that the self-driving car might soon be having problems. Furthermore, it could be that the roadway has a pothole and the self-driving car got damaged by hitting the pothole. The V2I might mention that the pothole has caused a problem. This could then be relayed by the V2I infrastructure to other AI self-driving cars that come along that roadway. Plus, hopefully, it would spur the roadway repair crews to fix the pothole make sure that it can no longer damage passing cars.

Besides using a knowledge-based system and a database to try and diagnose the car sounds, another approach would be via the use of Machine Learning (ML) and Deep Learning (DL).

If an entire fleet of AI self-driving cars are reporting various sounds and noises, along with the later-on determination by a car mechanics of what it signified, this kind of data could be used for pattern matching.

Using a large-scale or "deep" artificial neural network, we could feed this data into the ML or DL and see if it can train on the data.

By doing so, whenever an AI self-driving car perchance encounters such a sound or noise, the ML or DL could be used to more definitively diagnose it. This could either be an on-board ML or DL that is placed inside the AI self-driving car or might be a cloud-based version and the AI self-driving car would access it via OTA or the equivalent.

Conclusion

Bang. Hiss. Ping. Pop. Clunk. Clack. Buzz. Rumble. Screech.

If your car is making these sounds, and if it isn't because you are playing some music or having a wild party inside the car, you ought to consider what your car is trying to secretly tell you. Might be a loose fan belt. Maybe your brakes are wearing out. The muffler on your car might be busted. Your bumper might be dragging on the ground.

AI self-driving cars will have lots of sensors that are pointing outward to detect what is happening around the AI self-driving car. I've repeatedly called for AI self-driving cars to also be outfitted with more sensors for purposes of AI self-awareness. By this, I mean that the AI self-driving car needs to know its own internal status.

One important way to determine the status of the AI self-driving car will be via the sounds and noises that the car makes. Humans use those sounds and find them useful as a premonition or forewarning that something might soon go horribly awry. We ought to expect the AI to do the same.

With the AI doing sound detection, there is a good chance of boosting how these sounds will be dealt with. The AI self-driving car can be tracking how often the sound occurs, along with the circumstances such as going uphill or downhill, making turns or going straight ahead, speeding up or slowing down, and so on. With an advanced knowledge-based system, and perhaps Machine Learning or Deep Learning, when also combined with OTA, V2V, and V2I, we can substantially boost the diagnostic capabilities for AI self-driving cars.

It would also be hoped that this will further translate into safer driving by the AI system since it will be using essential clues in determining how best to safety drive the self-driving car. That's music to my ears, or, I might say are the sounds that I want to hear.

CHAPTER 6

NO SPEED LIMIT AUTOBAHN AND AI SELF-DRIVING CAR

CHAPTER 6

NO SPEED LIMIT AUTOBAHN

AND

AI SELF-DRIVING CAR

The joys of driving on the German autobahn!

Nearly two-thirds of the 8,100 miles of the autobahn system allow unrestricted speeds. This means that there is no speed limit. Go as fast as your heart desires. Go as fast are your car can go. Go as fast as your fears will let you proceed. I mention the fears part of this driving experience because there are some drivers that frankly are not so keen on driving at super high speeds and they either fear the consequences or at times have panic attacks about it.

I lived in Germany for a year and personally morphed through several mental and emotional states about the autobahn.

At first, I was quite excited about being able to drive at blazing speeds. Having come from the United States for my yearlong visit to Germany, I was well acquainted with the fact that mighty speeds were pretty much verboten in my home country.

Sure, I had occasionally had a lead foot as I drove from Southern California to the Las Vegas strip in Nevada, everyone drives fast through the desert areas that are merely an impediment to getting to the tables in Vegas and laying out some bets. But this over-the-top speeding came with the chance that you would get stopped by the police and it was as much a bet to get a ticket and a hefty speeding fine as were the odds of losing your savings while gambling in Vegas.

Believe it or not, I gradually kind of got used to the fast driving of the autobahn. Interestingly, I also discovered that I had my own threshold of how fast I was willing to go. I also discovered that there seems to always be someone wanting to go faster than you, no matter how fast you might think you are going. I would shake my head in disdain at cars that came up to my bumper, while each of us were both driving already at hyper speeds, and dutifully would try to get out of their way. It was surprising to see them scoot away from me and zoom ahead, given that I was already going at such a high speed, and I tried to guess how much faster they must be going to be such a blur.

The colleagues and friends that I had in Germany would tell me that the autobahn unrestricted speed limit was essentially a birthright. The oft repeated slogan is "Free travel for free people." This seemed to therefore intertwine with their culture and their psyche. You dare not try to take away their unrestricted speed. You would need to pry their dead cold hands from their steering wheel to try and do so, which I mention as a kind of nod to how some Americans perceive their rights related to guns.

One aspect about the autobahn that I admired was how well kept it seemed to be. One would hope that when trying to use a road for such high speeds that you would keep the road in decent shape. The dangers from potholes and other roadway surface issues are greatly magnified when you are traveling at tremendous speeds. The car will react instantaneously and the human driver might not be able to react as quickly, thus, any roadway imperfections can have a rather daunting result.

There were an estimated 400 people killed in autobahn car incidents last year. This number of course is unfortunate. When put in light though of the number of miles driven, the per capita basis is actually not statistically abysmal. With a population of around 83 million, and the number of cars in Germany estimated at 46 million, there are perhaps a total of 350B to possibly 385B miles traveled (often referred to as VMT, Vehicle Miles Traveled). The average number of miles driven per car is estimated around 8,300 miles.

When you take a look at charts of deaths per 100,000 people due to driving incidents, Germany is around 4.3, which is actually relatively low, and a lot less than the estimated 10.9 in the United States. The point of these numbers and statistics is that it doesn't seem that the unrestricted speeds of the autobahn are somehow leading to a vastly larger number of car related deaths. I've not seen any published numbers that are able to make the case that the autobahn is a magnet for car related deaths or otherwise pushes up the likelihoods of car deaths.

That being said, there are certainly some quite well-known consequences of the high speeds on the autobahn. Few would dispute the idea that when there is a car accident on the autobahn, the odds are that the results can be fairly horrifying. If a car spins out of control at hyper speed, it is going to cause some armor busting damage to anything nearby. Roadway railings will get bent out of shape. Other cars nearby are going to become pinball targets. And so on.

Another aspect is that there is a solid chance that when a car accident occurs, it can become a cascading one. Other cars that come upon an incident might not have sufficient time to slow down or otherwise react. They then can be caught up into the incident. A series of cars piling up can happen readily. The closest I've experienced in the United States has involved cars driving in the fog that cascade into each other when a car accident happens, and also sometimes I've seen the same happen when there is ice or snow on the roadways.

My colleagues and friends there in Germany emphasized to me that it was the responsibility of each driver to get out of the roadway as quickly as possible whenever having any car troubles. I recall one time that I was driving on the autobahn and had a colleague with me, and I saw dark smoke billowing up ahead. I started to slow down. My colleague looked at me with a puzzled expression and asked why I was slowing down. I told him that I wanted to be careful as we approached seemingly an adverse car accident up ahead (I assumed a car was likely on fire after a car crash of some kind).

He got irritated at me and insisted I proceed along at full speed. Why, I asked him? He assured me that the German driver that was up ahead would certainly get out of the way, as prescribed by law and by the accepted credo of drivers there. If I slowed down it would only likely cause me to get into a car accident because some other car from behind me would get confused about why I was slowing down. I admit this logic was a bit beyond my usual way of thinking and I wondered whether an injured or possibly dead driver in the perhaps car accident up ahead would really have been able to get off the road or not.

In any case, I did survive the autobahn experience while in Germany for the year and both enjoyed driving on the infamous autobahn and at times had some trepidations about it. One of those love-hate relationships, I suppose.

One aspect that was vividly brought to my attention was that the autobahn was a source of pride for the country. I don't know of any other place on earth that has this unrestricted speed limit for such a large geographical area of thousands of miles and that has somehow made it all work. Most of the locals did not particularly bring up the autobahn as a topic, since they take it for granted. It is there, it exists, it works, and they are happy with it.

They did point out that it acts as a tourist attraction. I am used to places like Disneyland in Southern California as being a tourist attraction, or perhaps Hollywood where you can see the movie stars. Thinking of the autobahn as a tourist destination was intriguing. I did meet a number of tourists that told me they might have not otherwise come to visit Germany except that they especially wanted to drive all out on the autobahn.

Besides the pride aspects and the tourist venue, there is also the factor that Germany makes cars. There is an image of German made cars that can zip along on the autobahn. This imagery is perhaps a significant element for why people worldwide desire to purchase German made cars. In that sense, you could say that the autobahn is intricately bound into the German economy. Car production and the selling of German cars might not do well if the autobahn did not have the unrestricted speed limit and the available branding that goes with it.

This discussion of the autobahn would not be complete if I didn't bring up an ongoing debate and concern within Germany about the unrestricted speed aspects. There is a storm of sorts brewing in Germany about the potential for a speed limit on the autobahn (note, as mentioned earlier, there are stretches that already do have speed limits, and so the debate is about potentially covering more or all of the autobahn with speed limits).

The debate is focused on pollution, rather than car safety aspects per se.

Turns out that the cars zooming along on the autobahn are pouring out carbon emissions. This butts up against the German led efforts to fight pollution and also their desire to be a leader in the climate change arena. The German Federal Environment Agency has suggested that by setting the speed limit to 75 miles per hour, the result could knock down carbon emissions by cars on the autobahn, decreasing the foul output by perhaps 9% per year. Generally, the floated speed limit number is around 75 to 80 miles per hour.

Geschwindigkeitsbeschränkung!

That's the lengthy German word meaning maximum speed limit. It's a word that for some Germans is a foul one, at least with respect to the autobahn. As mentioned earlier, the unrestricted speed is a key source of pride, it attracts tourists, it ties into the economy, it has merged into the culture and mindset of the people, and so anyone trying to mess with it is going to find themselves confronting quite a fierce resistance.

Some of my friends and colleagues felt that driving at 75 or 80 miles per hour is a type of insult. It is beneath anyone of proper driving ability. It also underuses the capability of the car. Why would you have a finely made precision car that can go much faster and yet limit it to being no more than a slowpoke on the roadways? They are sympathetic to the noxious emissions factor and regret that pollution is a byproduct, but they are not convinced that the speed limit imposition is the means to deal with the problem.

It's an internal political and public battle that can tear apart the best of friends and spark rather heated discussions. Seems like everyone has a diehard opinion on the matter.

What does this have to do with AI self-driving cars?

At the Cybernetic AI Self-Driving Car Institute, we are developing AI software for self-driving cars. One interesting question is whether or not AI self-driving cars might be driving on the autobahn at unrestricted speeds, and also whether the advent of AI self-driving cars might play into the future of the autobahn.

Allow me to elaborate.

I'd like to first clarify and introduce the notion that there are varying levels of AI self-driving cars. The topmost level is considered Level 5. A Level 5 self-driving car is one that is being driven by the AI and there is no human driver involved. For the design of Level 5 self-driving cars, the auto makers are even removing the gas pedal, brake pedal, and steering wheel, since those are contraptions used by human drivers. The Level 5 self-driving car is not being driven by a human and nor is there an expectation that a human driver will be present in the self-driving car. It's all on the shoulders of the AI to drive the car.

For self-driving cars less than a Level 5, there must be a human driver present in the car. The human driver is currently considered the responsible party for the acts of the car. The AI and the human driver are co-sharing the driving task. In spite of this co-sharing, the human is supposed to remain fully immersed into the driving task and be ready at all times to perform the driving task. I've repeatedly warned about the dangers of this co-sharing arrangement and predicted it will produce many untoward results.

Let's focus herein on the true Level 5 self-driving car. Much of the comments apply to the less than Level 5 self-driving cars too, but the fully autonomous AI self-driving car will receive the most attention in this discussion.

Here's the usual steps involved in the AI driving task:

- Sensor data collection and interpretation

- Sensor fusion

- Virtual world model updating

- AI action planning

- Car controls command issuance

Another key aspect of AI self-driving cars is that they will be driving on our roadways in the midst of human driven cars too. There are some pundits of AI self-driving cars that continually refer to a utopian world in which there are only AI self-driving cars on the public roads. Currently there are about 250+ million conventional cars in the United States alone, and those cars are not going to magically disappear or become true Level 5 AI self-driving cars overnight.

Indeed, the use of human driven cars will last for many years, likely many decades, and the advent of AI self-driving cars will occur while there are still human driven cars on the roads. This is a crucial point since this means that the AI of self-driving cars needs to be able to contend with not just other AI self-driving cars, but also contend with human driven cars. It is easy to envision a simplistic and rather unrealistic world in which all AI self-driving cars are politely interacting with each other and being civil about roadway interactions. That's not what is going to be happening for the foreseeable future. AI self-driving cars and human driven cars will need to be able to cope with each other.

Returning to the topic of the autobahn, let's consider the ways in which AI self-driving cars might come to play regarding the autobahn matter at-hand.

Let's start with the matter that has got many people up in arms about potentially putting a speed limit on the autobahn, namely the carbon emissions of cars that ride on the autobahn.

For AI self-driving cars, it is likely that most or nearly all AI self-driving cars will be EV's (Electrical Vehicles), and as such the tailpipe emissions issues goes away. Some argue that you need to calculate the emissions due to power plants that will produce the electrical energy needed for EVs, and perhaps add that to a per capita sense of "emissions" for EVs, but I'm not going to go that route herein. Let's generally say that the carbon emissions coming out of an EV car is zero.

Why would most or nearly all AI self-driving cars be EV's? Partially due to the aspect that the AI self-driving car is an electrical power guzzler of sorts, needing to use electrical power for the multitude of added sensors, the multitude of added computer processors, and other add-ons that make an AI self-driving car a functioning AI self-driving car. You can generate the power via conventional means and use a gasoline or diesel fueled engine, but it seems like it will be easier to go with an EV. There is also usually a gigantic battery in an EV, while the battery for a conventional car is typically puny.

Plus, there seems to be a hope that the advent of AI self-driving cars will persuade people to switch from gas guzzlers to EVs. Besides the EV being a natural fit due to the ability to generate the needed electrical power and have large-scale batteries on-board the car, the thinking is that if people want the AI self-driving car aspects, they might be more willing to switch to an EV if that's the type of vehicle being used for AI self-driving capabilities. This would help out the environment and reduce too a dependency on gasoline.

In a manner of speaking, the AI self-driving aspects might be the icing on the cake to get people over to EVs. Right now, there are only about 1% of all cars in the United States that are EVs, and so it is a tiny portion of the car population. Assuming that we aren't going to try and retrofit existing cars to be AI self-driving cars, it means people are going to be buying new cars. If they are going to be buying new cars, an incentive to buy an EV would be the AI self-driving capability.

The key point is that if we are going toward AI self-driving cars, eventually, inexorably, and if those AI self-driving cars are mainly EV's, it would seem to "solve" the autobahn qualm about the carbon emissions.

For Germany, they are faced with having to ascertain whether they believe that AI self-driving cars are coming or not, and if so, and assuming the use of EV's will then predominate, they could wait out the existing carbon emissions issue and be able to assuage it during the switchover to AI self-driving cars.

The question then becomes how much pollution they could have otherwise reduced in the interim by setting speed limits and does that amount of emissions reduction "payoff" for the consternation of restricting the speed limits of the autobahn until the arrival of AI self-driving cars.

Notice that this is a different approach to the matter. For most debates, the usual argument is to permanently set speed limits. In the case of this alternative argument, the question becomes the interim period rather than a forever kind of timeline.

For those that are pressing for the carbon emissions reduction, any furtherance of emissions is bad, and so they would say that the speed limit restrictions could be temporary, and this should satisfy the "no speed limits" proponents. Those proponents just need to keep their eye on the emergence of AI self-driving cars and once that happens, presumably the speed limit goes back to unrestricted.

For those that are vocal about keeping unrestricted speed limits, they would say that the lack of a speed limit should continue unabated and that the emissions contingent just needs to wait for the advent of AI self-driving cars. The problem of foul emissions, in a manner of thinking, will be going to solve itself, doing so without having to mess with the existing approaches such as speed limit aspects.

Get out your crystal ball because the interim period could either be short or long, depending upon how fast or slow you see the emergence of AI self-driving cars.

This takes us to another facet about AI self-driving cars and humans. One yet unresolved question is whether humans will be willing to give up their ability to drive a car. It could be that those that love to drive the autobahn do so because they relish being at the wheel. For a true Level 5 AI self-driving car, they won't be at the wheel, the AI will be.

As such, there might be a backlash by humans that cling to being able to drive. If that's the case, there will be an ongoing mix of human driven cars and AI self-driving cars. And if that's the case, those human driven cars might or might not be EV's. Thus, for any modeling you might want to do about carbon emissions from cars, you need to consider the holdouts and how many of those won't switch to an EV, regardless of whether the EV is an AI self-driving car or not.

So, do humans like the autobahn because the unrestricted speed gets them to where they are going faster, or do they have an innate desire to be driving at high speeds?

For those that are focused on getting to their destination faster, presumably being driven by the AI is fine with them. Furthermore, they can use the time in the AI self-driving car for other pursuits, such as taking meetings, playing games, being entertained, and so on. All in all, they would likely embrace the AI self-driving car.

Suppose that the autobahn does have unrestricted speeds when AI self-driving cars emerge. Should AI self-driving cars be going at unrestricted speeds?

This is not an axiomatic kind of question and answer. There are two sides to this coin.

One viewpoint is that it makes sense to have unrestricted speeds for AI self-driving cars. Assuming that the AI self-driving car is engineered for top speeds, the AI will presumably be able to dispassionately drive the self-driving car and not be vulnerable to the human driving foibles. The AI won't be getting drunk, at least not in the way that humans do. The AI won't get angry and have road rage, as humans do. And so on.

This implies that the AI will be a safer driver than humans and translates into less car crashes and less human deaths due to car crashes. For those that are somewhat fanatical and claim it will be zero fatalities, I try to bring them down to earth and point out that there are some car accidents that are unavoidable, no matter how good the AI self-driving car might be at driving. If a truck ahead of you dumps debris onto the roadway in front of your AI self-driving car, all bets are off. If the roadways have a mix of human driven cars and AI self-driving cars, all bets are off.

Admittedly, with the use of V2V (vehicle-to-vehicle) electronic communication, AI self-driving cars will have an added advantage about driving at high speeds. These AI self-driving cars equipped with V2V can send electronic messages to each other, trying to warn about debris ahead on the autobahn, or do so to coordinate their movements.

There is a chance that we'll have AI self-driving cars working in unison with each other. There are upcoming advances in swarm intelligence, namely having multiple entities that coordinate and collaborate, and this will further enhance driving on the autobahn. Whereas there are cascading car accidents today, the proper use of V2V among AI self-driving cars could likely reduce the chances of multiple cars getting caught up in any one particular incident.

Another plus for AI self-driving cars on the autobahn would be the emergence of V2I (vehicle-to-infrastructure) electronic communications.

This V2I involves the roadway infrastructure sending and receiving messages as AI self-driving cars zoom along the autobahn. The V2I could caution the AI self-driving cars to slow down because there is a wreck up ahead, or maybe give the green light to proceed at top speeds because the road is clear and steady.

It is hard to imagine that a human driver can drive as safely as a true Level 5 AI self-driving car that also has the added edge of using V2V and V2I. Of course, this notion of the true Level 5 AI self-driving car is only a notion right now, likewise the use of V2V and V2I on any scale is also only a notion. In that sense, this is all speculation about how AI self-driving cars will play out.

Speaking of which, do we know for sure that AI self-driving cars can indeed handle driving on an unrestricted speed limit basis?

Most of the auto makers and tech firms that are developing AI self-driving cars are focusing on having their AI self-driving cars drive at posted speed limit speeds. They want to make sure that their AI self-driving car can handle the usual speeds of say 65-75 miles per hour as a maximum. Along with making sure that the AI self-driving car can go at the school-zone speeds of 10 miles per hour and do so without harming people.

Worrying about letting the throttle loose and having your AI self-driving car proceed at blazing speeds is not much of a concern right now. Get the normal speeds tidied up first, and then take a look at how things go with the faster speeds.

You might be assuming that if the AI self-driving car does fine at say 65-75 miles per hour, wouldn't it also make sense that it must do well at 100 or 120 miles per hour too?

You'd be mistaken in that assumption.

The AI self-driving car has various sensors that are able to collect roadway data and process what is around the self-driving car. There are various timing aspects involved in those sensors and the interpretation of their data.

The AI self-driving car has a multitude of computer processors that undertake the sensor fusion, the virtual world model updating, the AI action planning, and the emitting of car controls commands. The car controls commands take time to be activated and carry out the commands.

This is all part of what I refer to as the "cognition timing" of the AI self-driving car. There are limits to how fast all of this processing can occur. The limits are based on what kinds of sensors you put onto and into the AI self-driving car. The limits are based on the kinds of computer processors you have on-board. The AI software and how it is tuned will impact the speeds of how quickly it can do its efforts.

Having an AI self-driving car that can cope with speeds of 65-75 miles per hour is handy, but it does not guarantee that at higher speeds things will still run well. It could be that the faster speed of the car will eclipse the processing speeds of the AI system. In that case, the car will be moving so fast that the AI cannot keep up with the task of properly driving the car. That's a recipe for disaster.

Don't mistake my points to suggest that an AI self-driving cannot handle ultra-fast car speeds. I am merely saying that the AI designers, AI developers, and everyone involved in making the AI system must come together and realize that they don't know for sure that everything will work at super-fast car speeds. They need to design for it. They need to test for it.

It isn't going to be something that occurs by happenstance, and nor would any of us want to have AI self-driving cars zipping along on the autobahn that we didn't believe could cope with the car speeds.

For the autobahn, the use of AI self-driving cars will potentially be a safer alternative than human driven cars, but it all depends on a slew of factors. Is the AI self-driving car properly established and tested at unrestricted speeds? Will the use of V2V and V2I take place in a manner that coincides with the advent of AI self-driving cars? Etc.

Back to the debate about the presumed interim period of dealing with the carbon emissions, some worry that if a so-called temporary imposition of speed limits on the autobahn is put in place, this won't be perhaps so temporary. It could be that once the speed limits are enacted, and even if AI self-driving cars arrive and are fine to drive at unrestricted speeds, those have that put the speed limits in place will insist to stick with the speed limits as so established.

Why would the speed limits potentially stay in place? One aspect is that even though AI self-driving cars are presumably going to be safer drivers than human drivers, I've pointed out that nonetheless there are still going to be some amount of car related crashes and human injuries or deaths associated with those car crashes.

If you assume that the car crashes are bound to be worse at the higher speeds, it could be that there is a sound argument to make sure the speed limits don't get removed (assuming they were put in place). Those proponents of the speed limits might say that since the country already accepted having speed limits, just keep it going, and this will save lives.

The counter-argument would be that at faster allowed speeds you could get to your destination sooner, and that the autobahn can allow for faster speeds. Usually, this argument gets overturned by the lives lost or lives saved argument. One can say that does it make a difference to get to your destination a few minutes earlier, but doing so has cost lives or injuries?

Conclusion

Should AI self-driving cars be allowed to drive at the unrestricted speeds of the autobahn?

We'll need to wait and see how well the AI systems are devised and tested to cope with the high-speed possibilities. In theory, if AI self-driving cars are properly developed and tested, and when accompanied by V2V and V2I, the AI self-driving car will be a boon to travel on the autobahn by a potential reduction in human-driven car accidents and in avoidance of cascading car crash circumstances.

The dilemma faced by Germany is whether to impose speed limits now, aiding in reducing the carbon emissions of cars on the autobahn right away, or wait until AI self-driving cars become prevalent (assuming too that such self-driving cars are mainly or completely EV's). I am sure there will be a lot of hand wringing over what to do.

Some would say that AI self-driving cars should be allowed to zoom, perhaps even taking the place of bullet trains and other fast mass transit options as a long-distance speedy option.

There are pundits that say that in the United States, once AI self-driving cars become prevalent, we ought to consider either raising our speed limits for longer stretches of highways, or possibly make those highways have unrestricted speed limits. Will the United States end-up with its own version of the autobahn, stretching from coast to coast? It all depends on how good the AI can be made to work. If AI did have emotions, I'm sure it would want the freedom to travel at the highest possible speeds and would "relish" being at the steering wheel in doing so.

CHAPTER 7

NOBLE CAUSE CORRUPTION

AND

AI SELF-DRIVING CARS

CHAPTER 7

NOBLE CAUSE CORRUPTION

AND

AI SELF-DRIVING CARS

Here's an age-old question for you, do the ends justify the means?

Some trace the origins of the question to the Latin collection *Heroides* as reportedly written by Ovid (Publius Ovidius Naso), namely it states "Exitus acta probat," which loosely translated could be interpreted as to whether the ends essentially prove or justify the means.

Most of us probably believe it came from the works of Machiavelli, and the question certainly fits for his essays known as *The Prince*. Indeed, one would assume that he would pose it not as a question and instead make it into an assertion, since his writing is about being conniving.

About the closest quote one can find in Machiavelli's classic writing is this: "Moreover, in the actions of men, and most of all Princes, where there is no tribunal which we can appeal, we look to results."

It's a bit of a stretch to say that this excerpt matches to the precise nature of the ends justifying the means, and perhaps might be saying that those that hold the keys will make the rules and therefore they can claim their aims are justified.

I am assuming that some of you would decry the entire notion that the ends justify the means. The implication of the notion is that you can do any darned untoward thing you want to do, as long as the ends that you are targeting are somehow noble.

I'd mildly object to the assumption that the ends being sought are of necessity noble, and it could be that the person arguing in favor of the ends justifying the means will want to convince themselves or us that the end is noble. I am saying that it might not really be. It could be a charade to make the means seem viable.

Let's test the logic involved. I will make you into a better person if I beat you silly. I do so under the auspices that what doesn't kill you will make you stronger (we keep hearing that one tossed around these days!). After you've been badly injured and permanently no longer have the use of your limbs and body, I declare that you are better off now and you should be thankful for my actions. It is hard to conjure up a circumstance wherein that after completely gutting you and barely keeping you alive, it has benefited you (we could try to craft some possibilities, but I dare say they would all pretty much be flimsy).

What sometimes happens is that people intending to do bad things will cleverly mask their upcoming bad deeds by wrapping it into a seemingly noble targeted ending. This generally allows them to get away with the bad things, since others will believe and at times rally in favor of the bad things, due to buying into the noble target ending that will presumably be someday reached.

Sometimes there are people that don't intend to do bad things, but fall into the pit of doing bad things, along the way to achieving what seems like a noble ending. Of course, it could also be that the noble ending was a facade all along.

The problem with all of this ends-and-means stuff is that you might not know what is true versus what is blarney.

Maybe the ends hoped for are true and good, while the means are good too. Or, the ends hoped for are true and good, while the means are rotten. Or, the ends are terrible, but made to seem like they will be good, and the means are good, while there's the other version which is the ends are terrible but made to seem like they are true and good, while the means are actually good.

Yikes, it can be confusing.

Those of you that might remember the *Dirty Harry* movies, it was the now-classic story of a cop that will do whatever it takes to get the criminal and illuminates this posture of the means justifying the ends. Get the bad guys at any cost. Break the law. Be as sneaky and dirty as might be necessary to win.

We see this theme repeatedly in modern-day TV shows and films. The movie *Taken* is another such example (spoiler alert!), wherein we cheer for the father trying to save his daughter, regardless of not just how many crooks need to first die, but even innocent bystanders might end-up as collateral damage. It's all okay, as long as the noble ends, in this case getting and expunging the dastardly criminals that have kidnapped his daughter and saving his daughter, remains the focus.

Can you remain a "good guy" and still break laws and possibly injure or kill innocents, assuming that your goal is something considered good?

This can be a difficult basis as justification. One can try to justify it, such as the master kidnapper in *Taken* is so horrible and possibly would continue on his horrific crime spree, so getting him killed is worth it, when you balance out the lives lost while trying to get him versus the grand total number of lives he might have injured or killed had he remained alive. A body count kind of rationalization.

Here's a more everyday example for you.

When I was a university professor, one my classes involved making use of a simulation to pretend you were running a business. Teams of students would each have a business assigned in the simulation and had to make executive decisions about the business. Weekly, the simulation would indicate how the businesses were faring, doing so by simulating the businesses trying to sell their products and competing against each other.

The grades in the class were greatly determined by how well each team's businesses made out in the simulation. The higher ranked your business was at the end of the simulation, the higher of a grade that went to your team. As you can imagine, the students were fiercely competing as they played the simulation. Members of each team typically pledged with their fellow team members that they would not speak to anyone else about their team strategy, for fear that it might get leaked to one of the other teams.

One of the teams decided to use a slightly different approach to win the simulation. They hacked it. By doing so, they were able to control the simulation results. They were cautious to make the simulation seem to still be working as expected. Cleverly, one might say, some weeks their team was not even in the top ranking. The hack was aimed to get them to the top pole position at the very end, and hopefully not arouse suspicion beforehand.

Turns out that their hack was discovered.

They claimed that their hack was justified. It was a means to an end. The end was to perform the best you could in the simulation. They found a means to do so. Nobody had said they could not do a hack. Yes, it was assumed that everyone would be using the simulation as intended, but there was not a specific declaration that you could not rig the simulation.

These students went even further and pointed out that in real-life, while in industry, there are all kinds of espionage taking place of one company spying on another company. In a sense, they were actually adding a real-world element to the simulation. This made the experience more powerful for everyone involved, they asserted.

What do you think, did their ends justify the means?

Another spoiler alert, the college did not.

There is a phrase given to those that believe they have a noble end and yet seemingly diverge from a proper means to reach it, namely the "noble cause corruption" phenomena.

What happens is that when someone might have an ends that they think is noble, they can become corrupted in the pursuit of that noble end. This can include carrying out unlawful acts, immoral acts, and whatever else might be needed to reach the desired ends.

In the news these days there is a colossal example in business of a presumed noble cause corruption case. It is the case of Theranos.

If you read any business-related news, you likely already know some aspects about the case. I'll go ahead and provide a quick recap about the major points. This is all well-documented in many big-time media outlets, and especially in an expose written by John Carreyrou of the Wall Street Journal and later further elaborated in his book entitled "Bad Blood: Secrets and Lies in a Silicon Valley Startup."

A Stanford University dropout, Elizabeth Holmes, at the age of 19, started a biotech firm named Theranos, and did so with the stated goal of being able to do a multitude of blood diagnostic tests via the use of a tiny drop or so of blood, using a single finger-prick device to get the blood. This seemed nearly impossible since you usually need to collect a much greater quantity of blood to do a multitude of tests, plus the kind of blood you get from a finger-prick is not as rich as you can get from using a conventional needle-in-the-arm to draw blood.

Her claims of being able to achieve these "ends" was a bold proclamation. It would change the world. Imagine how much easier and cheaper it could be to do blood tests. People would no longer need to fear taking a blood test. It could be done easily and just about anywhere. The blood-testing marketplace would be utterly disrupted and transformed. She went on a kind of public relations campaign for her company and the noble cause, holding the banner high, seeking to raise money and attention to her efforts.

Elizabeth became very practiced at presenting herself to the media. She combined a sense of humility with an indication of strength and confidence. She kept always hammering away at the ends and would shrewdly divert attention away from the means. She made the covers of some of the biggest media magazines. The story was like something out of a fairy tale. Young female entrepreneur, seeking to make the world a better place, and the media ate it up completely.

She got hundreds of millions of dollars in backing from some heavy weight investors, though few at the time seemed to realize that these investors were not biotech savvy. This likely helped the subterfuge. It is said that whenever anyone of biotech merit started to ask probing questions, Elizabeth and Theranos managed to avoid giving sufficient answers.

It turns out that the claimed technology did not exist and did not work as claimed. What makes the story especially notable is that Theranos did a deal with Walgreens and began actually performing the service for real people in selected cities in the United States. Sadly, many of the blood tests done turned out to be wrong. Indeed, over a million blood tests had be to revoked and redone. For any of you that happened to have taken one of those blood tests, it is unimaginable how you must feel, now knowing that what the blood test reported at the time was false or at best misleading. This impacted real people's lives in real ways.

Elizabeth and Theranos were charged with a massive fraud by the SEC, formally filed on March 14, 2018.

There are also criminal conspiracy and wire fraud charges that were leveled by the U.S. Attorney of the Northern District of California on June 15, 2018. Theranos ceased operations on August 31, 2018.

Some say that Elizabeth was a true believer in her cause and perchance got caught up in not being able to achieve the ends she desired. The means were not so good, but the targeted end was noble. Interviews with her defense attorney reveal that they are taking the stance that if she had not been so rudely and inappropriately interrupted in her quest, which therefore they contend shortchanged the time needed to perfect the technology, the ends would have been reached. It will be interesting to see how that "justification" plays out in the courtroom.

There are some that say that it was all a scam from day one. Those critics say that it must have been known by the founder and core team that what was being proposed was the equivalent of a perpetual motion machine.

No one in the media and nor the investors seemed to want to tell the king that maybe they weren't wearing any clothes. Critics say it was easier and sold more newspapers and magazines if the headlines were that this was a miracle come true, plus the investors were being portrayed as lucky they got in, while other investors could only look from afar and be jealous of not having had a chance to lay money on the line for Theranos.

There are lots of other details that are fascinating about the case. It truly is akin to a great fiction novel or movie script. One key aspect that helped it all unravel was that the grandson of one of the major investors got hired by the company, and he discovered what was really going on, which the firm then attempted to suppress him and he took a lot of gruff accordingly. Now he is an unsung hero.

What can the Theranos case tell us?

The bigger the noble ends, the likely easier it is to justify the means. The more too that the means can get out-of-hand without causing too much of a ruckus, because you just come back to the ends and everyone starts smiling again.

Let's switch the domain of focus and consider whether this kind of noble cause corruption can happen in the field of Artificial Intelligence (AI).

Yes, of course it can.

There are subtle ways this can arise, and other more apparent ways in which it can arise.

We've seen recently the concerns voiced toward the major tech and social media firms about their seeming lack of attention to privacy issues of AI systems and how they have either misled the public about the data being recorded or they have sold it or otherwise did not appear to be quite as careful about data privacy as many assumed they were.

Critics argue that there was an undertone of noble cause corruption involved in these cases.

If you are trying to bring AI-advanced social media and new tech to the world at large, well, something is going to break along the way, so say the tech firms. It is a noble end. The means maybe gets a bit jumbled along the way, but that's Okay, since the end is really good. In fact, as we all know, the tech industry relishes the credo that you need to break things to make progress, and if you aren't breaking enough things, and fast enough, you aren't doing enough.

Simply stated, the mantra has been "move fast, break things." Seems like we can include subliminally that the ends justify the means.

Let's take a look at another facet of this approach in AI.

There are some critics that worry we'll have massive unemployment among human workers by the emergence of AI systems. There are some AI devotees that say that's not their problem. They are merely technologists trying to extend AI. Take it for what it's worth, they retort. Some liken this attitude to a kind of noble cause corruption.

Those on the noble AI quest might argue that via whatever means possible, aiming to create true AI, and have an artificial form of intelligence, it is such a vaunted noble end, there is little need or concern about what might happen along the way to reach it.

Some critics at times refer to the emerging AI systems as a kind of Frankenstein problem. This is akin to the ends justifying the means. There are some too that are worried about a singularity and a backlash by the sentient AI toward all of humanity, though that's a bit farfetched in comparison to where AI really is today.

What does this have to do with AI self-driving cars?

At the Cybernetic AI Self-Driving Car Institute, we are developing AI software for self-driving cars. There are some industry critics that are concerned that there is a chance for some of the auto makers and tech firms to fall into the noble cause corruption basket as it applies to AI self-driving cars.

Allow me to elaborate.

I'd like to first clarify and introduce the notion that there are varying levels of AI self-driving cars. The topmost level is considered Level 5. A Level 5 self-driving car is one that is being driven by the AI and there is no human driver involved. For the design of Level 5 self-driving cars, the auto makers are even removing the gas pedal, brake pedal, and steering wheel, since those are contraptions used by human drivers. The Level 5 self-driving car is not being driven by a human and nor is there an expectation that a human driver will be present in the self-driving car. It's all on the shoulders of the AI to drive the car.

For self-driving cars less than a Level 5, there must be a human driver present in the car. The human driver is currently considered the responsible party for the acts of the car. The AI and the human driver are co-sharing the driving task. In spite of this co-sharing, the human is supposed to remain fully immersed into the driving task and be ready at all times to perform the driving task. I've repeatedly warned about the dangers of this co-sharing arrangement and predicted it will produce many untoward results.

Let's focus herein on the true Level 5 self-driving car. Much of the comments apply to the less than Level 5 self-driving cars too, but the fully autonomous AI self-driving car will receive the most attention in this discussion.

Here's the usual steps involved in the AI driving task:

- Sensor data collection and interpretation
- Sensor fusion
- Virtual world model updating
- AI action planning
- Car controls command issuance

Another key aspect of AI self-driving cars is that they will be driving on our roadways in the midst of human driven cars too. There are some pundits of AI self-driving cars that continually refer to a utopian world in which there are only AI self-driving cars on the public roads. Currently there are about 250+ million conventional cars in the United States alone, and those cars are not going to magically disappear or become true Level 5 AI self-driving cars overnight.

Indeed, the use of human driven cars will last for many years, likely many decades, and the advent of AI self-driving cars will occur while there are still human driven cars on the roads. This is a crucial point since this means that the AI of self-driving cars needs to be able to contend with not just other AI self-driving cars, but also contend with human driven cars. It is easy to envision a simplistic and rather unrealistic world in which all AI self-driving cars are politely interacting with each other and being civil about roadway interactions. That's not what is going to be happening for the foreseeable future. AI self-driving cars and human driven cars will need to be able to cope with each other.

Returning to the matter of the noble cause corruption and how it might apply to the AI self-driving car industry, let's consider some of the ways in which this might happen.

Suppose an AI developer is under-the-gun to get a Machine Learning (ML) or Deep Learning (DL) system to work that will be able to analyze visual images and find posted street signs in the images. For example, using a convolutional neural network to try and detect a stop sign or a speed limit sign. The AI developer amasses thousands of images that are used to train the deep or large-scale neural network. Feeding those images into the budding AI system, the AI developer tweaks it to try and ensure that it is able to spot the various posted street signs.

As I've stated in my writings and presentations at conferences, oftentimes these ML or DL are quite brittle. This brittleness means that there will be circumstances in which a visual image captured while an AI self-driving car is underway will maybe not be properly examined by the ML or DL that's been implemented and placed into the on-board car AI system.

The sensor data interpretation might state that there isn't a stop sign in the image, even though there really is one there, known as a false negative. Or, the sensor data interpretation might state that there is a stop sign in the image, even though there isn't one there, known as a false positive. These false indications can have a daunting and scary impact on the AI's efforts to drive the self-driving car.

Imagine that you are driving along and for whatever reason fail to see a stop sign and run right through the stop without any hesitation. I've seen this happen a few times during my years of driving. It takes your breath away when you see it happen.

The odds are that the driver might plow into someone or something and injure or kill someone, very frightening. You look in amazement when it happens and cannot believe what you just saw, especially if by luck no one gets hurt then you think it is a miracle that nothing adverse occurred.

The other case of falsely believing a stop sign exists when it does not, this too can potentially create a car crash or similar adverse event. If a car suddenly and seemingly inexplicably comes to a stop, there is a solid chance that a car behind might ram into the stopped car. I suppose if you had to choose between a car that doesn't stop at a real stop sign versus a car that stops at an imaginary stop sign, you'd feel "better" about the stopping at an imaginary stop sign, though it all depends upon the specifics of the traffic situation at the moment.

The AI developer that is crafting the convolutional neural network is pinched for time in terms of being able to fully test the system and has not yet vetted ways to avoid the false positives and false negatives. The AI developer was given a deadline and told that the latest iteration of the ML or DL needs to be pushed into the on-board self-driving car system right away. This can be done via OTA (Over-The-Air) electronic updating with the AI self-driving car.

This AI developer believes earnestly and with all their heart in the importance of AI self-driving cars. It is a noble end to ultimately be able achieve true AI self-driving cars.

Why?

Because it is believed that AI self-driving cars will save lives. People that are being killed daily in human driven car crashes are needlessly dying, since if we had AI self-driving cars there would not be such deaths, or so the pundits say (I refer to this as the "zero fatalities, zero chance" myth).

It is also a noble cause because of the mobility that will be spread throughout the world. People that do not have access to a car and getting around will be able to simply summon an AI self-driving car and be on their way. Some refer to this as the democratization of mobility.

There are other stated noble cause outcomes for the advent of AI self-driving cars and I won't go into all of them here. Generally, it is rather well-publicized that there are claimed noble ends to be had.

The AI developer has to make a choice between proceeding with the release of his convolutional neural network into the active AI self-driving car on-board system, though the AI developer knows it is not ready for prime time, but this AI developer is faced with the urgency of a deadline and been told that the failure to download the latest version will hold-up progress on the budding AI self-driving car being trial fielded.

What should the AI developer do?

The target end is a noble one. Being the inhibitor of reaching the noble end, well, that's a tough pill to swallow. In this case, the AI developer decides it is best to proceed with something, and not hold-up the bus, so to speak, and opts to go ahead and let loose the not-yet-ready convolutional neural network. Accordingly, the AI developers makes it download ready and pushes it along.

Noble cause corruption.

The AI developer felt compelled by the noble cause to proceed with something they knew wasn't ready and felt that the means was ultimately justifiable by the highly desirable ends. And though I've mentioned the instance of a visual image analyzer that fell under this spell, you should enlarge the scope and realize that any of the numerous AI subsystems could be equally pushed along and yet not be appropriately ready.

It could be the sensor elements involving the cameras, the radar, the ultrasonic, the LIDAR, and so on. This can also apply to the sensor fusion portion of the AI system.

It could readily apply to the virtual world model updating portion. There is an equal chance that the same fate might befall the AI action planning portion, and likewise could happen with the car controls commands subsystem.

The advent of AI self-driving cars carries such a tremendous notion of noble cause that it is tempting by some to justify otherwise untoward actions to try and make sure that AI self-driving cars come to fruition. If you are creating an AI system that maybe does something more pedantic, such as an AI system that can help you play a video game or perhaps aid you in shopping for groceries, these are not nearly as noble.

AI self-driving cars have the drop-the-microphone noble cause. These are AI systems that are about saving lives. These are the AI systems about changing the world and making lives better.

There aren't many AI systems that can claim that kind of double-whammy.

As earlier mentioned, the greater the noble ends, the chances of being slippery about the means will often be increased.

Conclusion

There is a clear and present danger that the alluring noble ends of reaching a true AI self-driving car can be corruptive toward the efforts involved in developing and fielding AI self-driving cars.

AI developers involved in AI self-driving car efforts are not necessarily plotting evil deeds (some conspiracy theorists believe they are), and instead can simply find themselves confronted with seemingly tough decisions about the work they are doing. Perhaps having to decide whether their decisions are justifiable as balanced against the desired ends.

I hope that AI developers and AI managers, along with all of those working at the various auto makers and tech firms that are devising AI self-driving cars, will take a moment to reflect upon whether there are any noble cause corruptive aspects involved in the efforts at their firm. If so, it is important to take the first step of recognizing the noble cause phenomena. Without realizing that the phenomena is or has taken over, you are less likely to be able to confront it.

Consider carefully the ends justifying the means, and make sure that you don't fall into the trap of believing that any means is acceptable as long as the goal of producing a true AI self-driving car is reached. I could translate that into Latin but having it in English seems sufficient.

CHAPTER 8
AI ROCKSTARS
AND
AI SELF-DRIVING CARS

CHAPTER 8

AI ROCKSTARS
AND
AI SELF-DRIVING CARS

Wanted, rockstar AI developer. You see this in numerous job ads these days. It doesn't say superstar. It doesn't say megastar. Instead, we seemed to have landed on using the now-so-popular rockstar moniker (though, some claim that it should be stated as two separate words, namely as "rock star" and that if you use "rockstar" you need to capitalize it to be "Rockstar" since this refers to a particular brand or trademark; confusing!).

Anyway, when you see such job ads, the question arises as to what the hiring firm and the hiring manager really are seeking to find.

It could be that the firm has no idea what a rockstar AI developer is or does. Instead, the company is hopeful of making the position itself seem more impressive, and a handy way to do so is to pump-up the volume surrounding the job ad. This might also make the firm appear loftier because they only hire the best of the best, and anything less than a "best best" (that's best squared) won't do.

You've got to wonder whether the firm has only and always hired these astounding AI rockstars, such that the entire AI team is, well, a bunch of rockstars. If so, whomever they hire will actually become just one of the motley crew, as they will be one among many of the vaunted AI rockstars. Might be disappointing for that new hire to realize they are now actually a run-of-the-mill rockstar when in the midst of a sizzling pool of all AI rockstars.

Or, it could be that the firm has never hired an AI rockstar and in this case they are hoping, no say begging, or make it beseech that they must have in their midst an AI rockstar developer. If they could just get one of these, akin to finding a unicorn, it would make all the difference in their AI efforts. The expectation perhaps is that the hired AI rockstar will leap tall buildings with a single bound and turn AI lackluster projects into golden nuggets of grandiose AI.

In talking with various firms that have been looking for an AI rockstar developer, which I often get asked for recommendations, I often find that the hiring manager didn't actually put into the job requisition that they were seeking a rockstar. They indicated in flatter and less flashy terms the nature of the position requirements. The HR (Human Resources) team, sometimes nowadays referred to as the Talent Management group, opted to add the rockstar indication when they posted the position for the world to see.

Why? As earlier suggested, they did so partially to make the position standout amongst the clutter of AI wanted job ads. Secondly, they also did so because they figured they would otherwise get inundated with applicants that barely know how to spell AI.

See, what's happening now is that everyone and their brother or sister wants into these AI jobs, which makes career sense due to the hefty pay premium and the belief that you are changing the world, but this also causes job seekers to perhaps stretch their AI savviness a tad.

By planting the AI rockstar proclamation as a flag of announcement in a job ad, HR hopes that it will discourage the AI unwashed, particularly those that decide they want to apply for the job and yet aren't up-to-par by the perceived AI stupendous standards of the HR team. It also makes things easier to turn down many that arise in the flood of applicants, due to merely being able to say that you aren't an AI rockstar. You might be an AI newbie, or you might be an

AI apprentice, or possibly even a seasoned AI specialist, and yet that's not necessarily what these firms think they want to hire.

The funny thing is that some of these firms want someone with on-the-job AI developer experience of 10 to 20 years, meanwhile they have a tendency to screen out someone that they believe has over-the-hill AI experience. It can be a Catch-22 for some of those AI developers that were busy and had their hands full during the earlier heyday of AI. Those AI developers had to go into hibernation or hiding during the AI winter that came along. With the advent of the AI spring, they polished up their resumes and aimed to get back into the AI game. Turns out, it's not so easy to do.

Admittedly, getting a true AI rockstar can be quite advantageous.

First, it allows the firm to tout the kind of talent they attract. Look at us, it says, given the fierce competition for the top 1% of AI developers, we got one. Obviously, our firm is on the cutting edge, they would then tout. We are the place to be and the proof is in the pudding, we got a big fish.

This is especially the gambit of the smaller firms or startups. They know that the bigger tech firms can readily attract these top enders. When the name of the firm is one that everyone knows, and one that already has an outstanding reputation, it is tough to compete when you are an unknown firm with an unknown future and with an unknown product.

Secondly, in my experience as a manager and leader, I've found that there is absolutely a difference in capability, effectiveness, and productivity between an average AI developer and an outstanding AI developer. There is no question that the outstanding AI developer is going to outperform the average AI developer. And not just by some minor incremental amount, instead more like an exponential amount.

In fact, at some points during my tenure as a corporate top executive, I've had to go to battle with HR over getting higher pay to acquire an outstanding AI developer.

In the minds of some HR folks, they think that the outstanding AI developer is worth maybe a handful of percentage points more in pay than the average one. I usually need to go around this logic and try to explain that giving a sizable boost in pay is readily going to payoff many times over. I say this because of the gigantic return for value that you get with the outstanding AI developers.

I am not knocking the average AI developers. They are good to have. They get their jobs done. They grind out the work. Yet, if I could have at least one or more of the outstanding AI developers mixed into the pack, it would be huge game changer for what the AI team can accomplish.

Don't be fooled though into thinking that if you toss one outstanding AI developer into a group of everyday AI developers that magic will somehow materialize. Not so.

There is a solid chance that some of the everyday AI developers will resent the outstanding AI developer. What makes the AI rockstar so revered, will be a common refrain. Let's see what magic touch this person has. Some of the other AI developers will take potshots at the outstanding AI developer. The existing AI team members might refuse to share their code or might make it hard for the new-hire to come up-to-speed by acting mum, justifying this by saying that if the person is that good, they should be able to figure out things on their own.

This in my book comes down to the lot of the AI manager or leader. If they aren't doing their job properly, they are going to make a mess of the AI talent that is amassed, likely whether there are any AI rockstars or not (and, worse so when there is an AI rockstar, since the odds are the rockstar will not be leveraged appropriately).

Indeed, I've seen some really topnotch AI teams that got completely kabobbed because the head of the AI team had no clue about how to actually manage or lead such a team. In some cases, they just tossed everyone together and figured it would coalesce, and in other cases they did so many Dilbert-like senseless management acts that the AI team was utterly counterproductive, in spite of the great talent that had been put together.

The nature of the AI rockstar also obviously makes a big difference too. If the top ender decides to act like they are there to save the day, it's going to likely rub others of the AI team the wrong way. By the snooty nose and the walking on water attitude, there are some AI rockstars that limit what you can do with them. Yes, they might have great raw AI talent as a skillset, but from a working-with-people perspective, they are a loser.

I remember one AI team that landed a top AI rockstar and the first thing the person did was opt to takeover the entire AI project that was floundering. Sure, it was handy that they had someone that might know how to turnaround the effort, but this rockstar decided that nobody but themselves was capable to get the ship righted. Instant alienation with the rest of the team.

Once again, I put this squarely on the AI manager. When I spoke with the AI manager, it was obvious that they were in a panic and could not figure out how to get themselves out of a pickle. They assumed that this AI rockstar would do it all. By putting his own head into the sand, the AI manager was praying that a miracle would occur by giving over the AI project to the rockstar.

The problem often times is that the AI rockstar is not a manger. This kind of makes sense because they are usually being hired as an individual contributor, a heads-down developer. They are not being hired to be a manager. Thus, the actual AI manager was handing over the AI project keys to someone that wasn't able to manage (of course, apparently neither was the anointed manager!).

I wrestle with some companies that want an AI rockstar and haven't yet figured out what they really need, in the sense of do they need someone that has the highly technical AI skills and want to apply those to the effort, or do they want someone that will manage a team of AI developers? Those are two different things.

I'm not saying that you cannot be a highly technical AI developer and also be a manager. What makes the issue confounding is when a firm that is doing the hiring hasn't figured out what they want or need. The firm might think it needs just the topnotch AI developer with pure technical skills, and meanwhile are blind to the aspect that they actually need someone either also with managerial skills or perhaps need another position made available of AI manger (or, they need to do something about an existing AI manager that maybe isn't right for the role).

Ideally, if you are looking for an AI rockstar developer that is purely a developer, the position actually matches to that need, and furthermore there is an AI team manager that knows how to properly make use of that talent. This usage includes how to marry the AI rockstar into the team and ensure that the AI team works collaboratively and as a well-managed team is supposed to do.

Let's suppose you do hire an AI rockstar and you well-integrate them into the AI team. That's a good start.

There are some aspects that can occur to regrettably undermine things.

One frequent pattern is that the other members of the AI team will be looking to the rockstar as someone that can be a kind of unstated mentor. You could say that's a positive sign that the rest of the AI team has taken to accepting and hopefully embracing the added AI rockstar.

What can happen though is that the AI rockstar, wanting to be part of the AI team and desirous of being collaborative (there are some that want this!), they will begin to allow these semi-mentoring relationships to build. Gradually, the AI rockstar is spending a sizable chunk of their time helping out the other AI team members.

I recall one AI rockstar that offered to do lunch-time brown bag sessions on the latest techniques for Machine Learning and Deep Learning, doing so because they had kept getting asked questions by individual members of the AI team. Rather than continuing to answer the questions one at a time, the rockstar realized it would be more efficient to do a voluntary lunch-time workshop series and get things done as a group rather than on an individual at a time basis.

This expanded into an after-work series too, taking place in the evenings. Gradually, the AI rockstar was becoming mired in trying to do the "right thing," namely helping the fellow AI team members, and yet was becoming overloaded in doing so. The AI manager was at first unaware of the extra effort being undertaken by the AI rockstar (that's one strike against the AI manager, since the manager ought to know when this is taking place).

When I entered into the picture, the AI manager told me that the AI rockstar was working out really well. The rest of the team loved the rockstar. The rockstar was excited to be able to share what they knew with the rest of the AI team.

Here's though the rub. When I spoke with the AI rockstar, the person was exhausted, and they told me privately that this added part of the job was beyond what they had expected. Was it really their job duty to do this kind of bend-over-backwards non-stop assistance for the rest of the AI team?

The rockstar said they weren't complaining, but that they were now working 40 to 50 hours on their regular work and putting in an additional 15+ hours per week on these added efforts. It was unrecognized by anyone else officially. Unofficially, the rest of the AI team was thanking the rockstar and bringing in free pizza and other goodies as a show of appreciation. The AI manager was clueless that the rockstar was suffering under the weight of trying to help the AI team members and simultaneously do they job they were presumably hired to do (let's make that strike two against the AI manager).

In this case, the AI rockstar was so flummoxed by the situation that they were secretly seeking to reawaken another job opportunity elsewhere that had fallen by the wayside when they took this job.

You might be puzzled as to why the rockstar did not just go talk with the AI manager and explain the extracurricular efforts? The rockstar didn't want to be a "tattletale" about the other AI team members, worrying that it might reflect poorly on them. The easiest "solution" seemed to be to find a job elsewhere and say that they had loved the job here but got a better offer and wanted to take it.

I'd say that this particular AI rockstar developer was a rarity. More often, the rockstar is one that has no bones about saying whatever they feel like saying. I knew one that would gladly tell a fellow AI team member that they were as dumb as a rock. This was done repeatedly and in front of other members of the AI team. Such a rockstar might either be unaware of the brashness and insulting nature of their demeanor, or they sometimes relish it and enjoy brandishing it.

This brings up one aspect that I admit gets my goat whenever it arises. I call it the jerk-rockstar causality confusion.

That's a mouthful.

Allow me to give you an example. One firm was trying to hire an AI rockstar and they brought me into the hiring process to help vet candidates.

They already had two finalists. One of the finalists was a real jerk. You could discern this the moment you spoke to the person. They were full of themselves, they acted like they could part the sea, and when I asked some fundamental AI questions as means to gauge what they really knew, the person immediately rejected them as beneath them and refused to answer the questions. The other candidate was more moderate and nearly reasonable, especially in contrast to the complete jerk candidate.

After I spoke with the two finalists, I went over and chatted with HR. The recruiter on the HR team said that the candidate that was "at times difficult" was clearly the better candidate and wanted to know what I thought. I asked how the recruiter assessed that the "at times difficult" candidate (i.e., the jerk) was the better of the two candidates?

Answer: Because AI rockstars are jerks and since the one candidate was a jerk, it meant the candidate was better than the other candidate (the one that was not so much of a jerk).

Say what? Apparently, there is a causality that if you are a jerk, ergo you are an AI rockstar. Likewise, presumably, if you are not a jerk, ergo you are not an AI rockstar.

Some AI rockstars have actually figured out this mindset exists and therefore they ramp-up the jerk factor when they meet people or are trying to get hired. They realize that as a society, we seem to have bought into the notion that the brilliant people are jerks (consider various TV shows and movies that depict this stereotype). I guess the assumption is that they are so brilliant that they didn't have the time or inclination to try and not be a jerk. Or, maybe being a jerk is a human default and the brilliant ones let the natural jerk shine through.

In any case, I mention this gets my goat because there are AI rockstar developers that are not jerks. I vehemently disagree with the thinking that being a jerk means you are a rockstar, and also, I vehemently disagree that not being a jerk means you are not a rockstar. I suppose if you want to go by a statistical factor, more often than not the rockstar is potentially going to be a jerk, but I wouldn't therefore set my sights on thinking that the jerk level is a sign that the rockstar is a rockstar.

As a quick recap on this diatribe about AI rockstars, they do exist, they are worth their weight in silver, they are not necessarily jerks, they can enhance an AI team, they can bring a glow to a firm that lands them, the "title" can be an attractor for a rockstar that wants to be recognized for what they can bring to the table, it can be a handy means of weening out the non-rockstars, and it can be harder than it might seem to discern whether someone is a true AI rockstar.

Even if you get yourself an AI rockstar developer, you can't just plop them into an AI project and an AI team and assume that the world will be wonderful. There needs to be an AI manager savvy enough to know how to leverage the capabilities of the AI rockstar. In some cases, the AI manager might need to rein in the jerk-aspects of a rockstar and harness it. In some cases, the AI manager might need to deal with others on the AI team that either wrongfully or rightfully might resent having the AI rockstar.

Furthermore, the AI manager has to be watching for signs that the AI rockstar is being pulled into too many directions at once. This can be exhausting for the rockstar, producing burnout, potentially undermining their rockstar skills, and might end-up with them leaving. They are a resource for the AI projects and usually aren't accompanied by their own self-managing skills.

If you want an AI rockstar that is both high technical and going to be doing development, plus you want them to be an AI manager, you need to realize these are two different roles combined into one.

Did you make it clear cut in the job description what you expect in the role in terms of the potential mixture of developer and manager in the AI rockstar? Does the hiring manager realize this? Does HR understand this? Are you making sure the candidate's matchup to both sides of that coin?

Realistically, too, how much time of the AI job consists of doing the development versus doing the managing? Often, the managing part is given short shrift and enormously underestimated. If so, it's a problem that will rear its ugly head once the AI rockstar comes on-board and gets underway.

You might believe that the managing side of things is say at most 3-5 hours per week of the rockstar's time, but the reality could be that it chews up half or more of their time. It is a common mistake to assume that managing is a trivial task and one that requires either no real skills or not much time.

I'd say the opposite is true, namely it requires some real topnotch skills and it will definitely consume a lot of time. In spite of the many jokes often made about management and managers, done properly it is a sight to see, and AI projects will arrive on-target and tend to avoid the disastrous results that most AI projects usually befall. Good AI managers are worth their weight in gold.

What does this have to do with AI self-driving cars?

At the Cybernetic AI Self-Driving Car Institute, we are developing AI software for self-driving cars. We and everyone else involved in AI self-driving cars such as the auto makers and various tech firms are all on the hunt for AI rockstar developers, plus we are often asked to aid in the identification, selection, hiring, and onboarding process.

Allow me to elaborate how this pertains to AI self-driving car efforts.

I'd like to first clarify and introduce the notion that there are varying levels of AI self-driving cars. The topmost level is considered Level 5. A Level 5 self-driving car is one that is being driven by the AI and there is no human driver involved. For the design of Level 5 self-driving cars, the auto makers are even removing the gas pedal, brake pedal, and steering wheel, since those are contraptions used by human drivers. The Level 5 self-driving car is not being driven by a human and nor is there an expectation that a human driver will be present in the self-driving car. It's all on the shoulders of the AI to drive the car.

For self-driving cars less than a Level 5, there must be a human driver present in the car. The human driver is currently considered the responsible party for the acts of the car. The AI and the human driver are co-sharing the driving task. In spite of this co-sharing, the human is supposed to remain fully immersed into the driving task and be ready at all times to perform the driving task. I've repeatedly warned about the dangers of this co-sharing arrangement and predicted it will produce many untoward results.

Let's focus herein on the true Level 5 self-driving car. Much of the comments apply to the less than Level 5 self-driving cars too, but the fully autonomous AI self-driving car will receive the most attention in this discussion.

Here's the usual steps involved in the AI driving task:

- Sensor data collection and interpretation

- Sensor fusion

- Virtual world model updating

- AI action planning

- Car controls command issuance

Another key aspect of AI self-driving cars is that they will be driving on our roadways in the midst of human driven cars too. There are some pundits of AI self-driving cars that continually refer to a utopian world in which there are only AI self-driving cars on the public roads. Currently there are about 250+ million conventional cars in the United States alone, and those cars are not going to magically disappear or become true Level 5 AI self-driving cars overnight.

Indeed, the use of human driven cars will last for many years, likely many decades, and the advent of AI self-driving cars will occur while there are still human driven cars on the roads. This is a crucial point since this means that the AI of self-driving cars needs to be able to contend with not just other AI self-driving cars, but also contend with human driven cars. It is easy to envision a simplistic and rather unrealistic world in which all AI self-driving cars are politely interacting with each other and being civil about roadway interactions. That's not what is going to be happening for the foreseeable future. AI self-driving cars and human driven cars will need to be able to cope with each other.

Returning to the topic of AI rockstar developers, let's consider how these rockstars are manifested in the context of the AI self-driving car industry.

If you were looking for an AI rockstar developer that has AI self-driving car expertise, where would you look? By-and-large, many of these AI developers have been sourced out of various university research programs that have had a focus on autonomous vehicles.

Indeed, many of the key AI self-driving car specialists and leaders of today that are at the major auto makers and tech firms developing AI self-driving cars came out of the DARPA (Defense Advanced Research Projects Agency) Grand Challenges that took place in the early 2000s.

In 2004, the first of the DARPA Grand Challenges took place, involving a race in the Mojave Desert that generally parallels Interstate 15 in California and required trying to make a 150-mile journey with an autonomous vehicle in the desert. Though none of the vehicles were able to successfully complete the race, and did not win the coveted $1 million cash prize, this effort approved by the U.S. Congress was able to kick-up further interest in creating AI self-driving cars.

Then in 2005, there were five winning autonomous vehicles, arriving at the finish line in this order, and for which I indicate the name of the vehicle and who provided it: (1) Stanley of the Stanford Racing Team, (2) Sandstorm of the Red Team from CMU, (3) H1hglander of the Red Team from CMU, (4) Kat-5 of the Team Gray from The Gray Insurance Company, and (5) TerraMax of the Team TerraMax of the Oshkosh Truck Corporation.

At the time, there was some criticism that these accomplishments were impressive but not overwhelming due to the nature of the driving environment. Some pointed out that driving in a desert is not the same as driving in a city or suburb setting. Though you might have a few desert tortoises or scary sagebrush, attempting to drive in a relatively barren scene is unlike being faced with other nearby cars, roadway aspects, pedestrians, and the like in an urban setting.

For 2007, the third DARPA Grand Challenge took place in a closed-track urban-like setup setting and became famously known as the "Urban Challenge." This took place at an Air Force Base in Victorville, California. Six of the submitted autonomous vehicles were able to complete the course, which included having to abide by various traffic related rules that has been stated.

That was over a dozen years ago. When the rush toward AI self-driving cars began just a few years ago commercially, many of those that had been directly or indirectly involved in the DARPA Grand Challenges either flocked to private industry or were lured out of universities into commercial enterprises. Some in the university settings opted to start their own firms or chose to try and remain in the academic world while splitting their time with being involved in the commercial efforts outside the gates of the university.

In any case, the point being that there has been an initial influx of AI rockstar developers from numerous university related AI self-driving car efforts.

I'm one of those.

But there are only so many of those such AI developers and it is insufficient as a pool for the number needed to fully resource the numerous and varied AI self-driving car efforts underway. As a result, there are now some being lured out of university research programs that were not around during the days of the DARPA Grand Challenge. These are researchers that came along after those days.

Another variant is that many universities are now doing research in autonomous vehicles of all kinds, including autonomous flying drones, autonomous flying planes, autonomous flying cars, autonomous submersible submarines, autonomous surface going boats, etc. This gives a wider choice of the kinds of AI developers that one might tap into when seeking AI specialists related to AI self-driving cars.

Those that have been in the automotive industry for a long time and have worked on ADAS (Advanced Driver Assistance Systems) are a potential pool of AI developers. They tend to have some strong skills on the automotive side and know well the inner elements of car-related systems and system standards. What they often lack is a strength in AI. Some of them have attempted to bolster their AI awareness by taking AI courses and otherwise supplementing their capabilities accordingly.

We are also on the verge of seeing poaching or the musical chairs game of AI developers hopping from one AI self-driving car effort to another. This hasn't happened too much just yet, partially due to the aspect that many of these efforts are still relatively new. There is also the sometimes golden handcuffs that firms use to try and keep their AI developers from jumping ship to another firm. I've predicted that we'll soon see more and more of movement between the AI self-driving car efforts.

We've been helping to train those that are somewhat versed overall in AI about the aspects of AI self-driving cars, though it is a steep hill to climb if the person doesn't have already some kind of relatively in-depth real-time systems experience.

AI self-driving cars and their systems all work in a very tight time constrained setting and involve the core aspects of real-time systems, plus these are real-time systems involving multi-ton cars that can bring about life-or-death.

In aiding the interviewing and selection process for some of the AI self-driving car searches for AI rockstars, one aspect that repeatedly comes across is the often-seen dogmatic perspective. It is somewhat common that a person versed in AI and self-driving cars or autonomous vehicles might have a particular bend or strongly wedded approach or technology that they adhere to.

This is akin to a computer programmer that insists on using a particular programming language and refuses to consider any other coding languages. Or, one that insists on using a particular software package or has opted to place all their eggs into one basket, and knows only that particular package, therefore they claim that it is the only and best way to go.

I recall one potential AI rockstar candidate that insisted cameras were the best way to collect sensory data for an AI self-driving car and eschewed the use of LIDAR. This candidate was absolutely convinced that LIDAR was overly expensive and not worth the effort to include in an AI self-driving car. Sidenote, I refer to this as the "myopic" or cyclops view of AI self-driving cars, wherein a person believes there is only one way that things are to be done.

What was especially interesting, and revealing was that the person had spent their entire prior efforts on traditional vision processing involving cameras. They had put at most a token effort towards learning about LIDAR. In that case, this "expert" had really had little basis for offering such a strong opinion of the tradeoffs between the two.

I also tried to point out that there is a rapid pace at which LIDAR costs are coming down, simultaneously the accuracy and features are rapidly increasing.

I also pointed out that this seemed to be a potentially false "mutually exclusive" type of debate. Does one necessarily need to choose between using cameras versus using LIDAR? Most of the AI self-driving car efforts to-date are using both (though, Tesla is a notable exception, and I've warned many times that I believe Elon Musk's claim that LIDAR won't be needed is sadly misguided and he'll eventually regret the choice, which he has even stated might turnout to be the case).

This potential AI rockstar was surprised to be challenged on this point about the cameras versus LIDAR matter. To-date, he had been able to browbeat most interviewers into submission by using arcane jargon and attempting to bolster his argument about cameras, which really was an argument about why he should be hired. I'm not saying that he lied, and I do believe he sincerely believed in the cameras approach, but I am saying that his lack of awareness and coupled with his personal bias is what led to his insistence.

I would also say this was another example of the jerk-rockstar causality confusion. Those that had interviewed the candidate liked the sense of confidence and spirit of the person and though there was an underlying know-it-all and jerk factor, this merely added to the person's glow that they must be an AI rockstar.

When I spoke with some of the executives and the hiring manager, I emphasized that since the firm was already using LIDAR, they were going to be bringing into their midst someone that was adamantly opposed to this part of their strategy and efforts. I was told that they would just keep the person in the cameras and vision processing team. No need to have them deal with the LIDAR team.

Sigh. I tried to point out that if they wanted to ensure a war between their teams, they certainly could so proceed. At every turn, this person would likely try to undermine the other team. The other team would likely become antagonistic toward the cameras team and if there wasn't bad blood yet, the company would soon be bathed in bad blood. This didn't seem to be a smart way to try and seamlessly craft an AI systems for which all of the parts need to work coherently and cohesively.

This does bring up another facet about AI rockstar developers in the AI self-driving car niche.

Typically, these AI rockstars have a specific and narrow area of skills and technology attention. That's fine, as long as this is realized and leveraged. Someone that is highly skilled at the sensors part of self-driving cars might not be familiar with the car controls aspects. Thus, you cannot just slam dunk someone into the car controls side if you've hired them based on their sensor-focused skills.

I also forewarn to be on the watch for a kind of technological bigotry, such as the candidate that was so convinced that cameras rule the world. It's handy for someone to be passionate about their area of expertise, but it is another thing when they bash another area of technology and want to fight against it. That's where you are bound to have problems arise and it will likely shakeup any AI team.

I'll cover a few other salient points about potential AI rockstars and self-driving cars.

One point is that they sometimes are so strongly opinionated that when they get onboarded and have a chance to look under-the-hood of the AI systems being developed, they can suddenly decide that everything is wrong and that there should be a do-over.

That can be quite a shock to the firm.

If the AI rockstar is actually right and they have discovered that there are serious and severe flaws, well, okay, thankfully they have found this, preferably before the firm has gotten too far along on their AI self-driving car efforts. On the other hand, if they person is being a jerk and merely spouting out false failings, maybe to boost their own sense of importance, or perhaps based on a misjudging of what they've found, it is going to likely cause chaos.

Imagine a firm that has invested perhaps millions upon millions of dollars into their AI self-driving car development, along with multitudes of expensive AI developer time and effort, and have someone that walks in the door and proclaims that it is a waste. Yikes! The newly hired AI rockstar will likely get heard because it is assumed that they are an AI rockstar, since they got hired under those auspices, and so it will be difficult to quiet down such a charge.

This could take the firm in a path that will last for weeks or months of internal handwringing and debate. All of which might be warranted, or might be a false "the sky is falling" and that drains the attention and monies of the firm. With the frenetic pace of AI self-driving car efforts, and the desire to keep ahead of the other AI self-driving car firms, getting bogged down in an acrimonious internal debate that perhaps has no basis will be draining and likely cause the firm to fall behind.

I don't want to suggest that the AI rockstar is necessarily wrong if they do find problems. In fact, it could be that others within the AI team have had qualms about the AI system, but they were either unsure of how to voice those qualms or felt they would not be heard if they did.

Internal naysayers are often cast aside and gain little by coming forth, other than a personal sense of doing what they believe to be right. When a newly hired AI rockstar opts to rock-the-boat, it can be an opportunity for suppressed members of the AI team to voice their concerns.

Conclusion

Everyone wants to hire a rockstar. And, why not? The implication is that if you are hiring someone less than a rockstar, you are presumably settling for the mediocre. What firm wants to run job ads saying they want to hire mediocre AI developers? Imagine the reaction. It would hurt the firm's reputation in the industry and it would likely have the internal AI teams feel like they have also been slapped in the face.

What exactly constitutes being an AI rockstar? Is it the number of years' experience in developing AI systems? Is it the kind of AI systems developed? Is it the prominence among your AI peers and within the AI community? In one sense, an AI rockstar status is in the eye of the beholder.

Some believe that AI rockstar labeling might be gradually running thin. Critics would say that it is akin to how school children are all told they are winners when playing a sport, even though they were participants and did not necessarily place in the top three or top five positions. Maybe everyone that does AI wants to believe they are an all-out super-duper AI rockstar. In that case, the search for AI rockstars is going to be easy, pick anyone that knows AI.

In any case, I advise firms to be mindful that when hiring an AI rockstar they ought to be carefully considering how the person will fit into their existing AI team. Furthermore, there needs to be a solid AI manager overseeing and managing the AI team, otherwise adding the AI rockstar could inadvertently cause the AI team to get waylaid or go kilter. It takes a village to make an AI self-driving car and hiring one AI rockstar as a solo act is not going to get you there.

APPENDIX

APPENDIX A
TEACHING WITH THIS MATERIAL

The material in this book can be readily used either as a supplemental to other content for a class, or it can also be used as a core set of textbook material for a specialized class. Classes where this material is most likely used include any classes at the college or university level that want to augment the class by offering thought provoking and educational essays about AI and self-driving cars.

In particular, here are some aspects for class use:

o   <u>Computer Science</u>. Studying AI, autonomous vehicles, etc.

o   <u>Business</u>. Exploring technology and it adoption for business.

o   <u>Sociology</u>. Sociological views on the adoption and advancement of technology.

Specialized classes at the undergraduate and graduate level can also make use of this material.

For each chapter, consider whether you think the chapter provides material relevant to your course topic. There is plenty of opportunity to get the students thinking about the topic and force them to decide whether they agree or disagree with the points offered and positions taken. I would also encourage you to have the students do additional research beyond the chapter material presented (I provide next some suggested assignments they can do).

RESEARCH ASSIGNMENTS ON THESE TOPICS

Your students can find background material on these topics, doing so in various business and technical publications. I list below the top ranked AI related journals. For business publications, I would suggest the usual culprits such as the Harvard Business Review, Forbes, Fortune, WSJ, and the like.

Here are some suggestions of homework or projects that you could assign to students:

a) <u>Assignment for foundational AI research topic</u>: Research and prepare a paper and a presentation on a specific aspect of Deep AI, Machine Learning, ANN, etc. The paper should cite at least 3 reputable sources. Compare and contrast to what has been stated in this book.

b) <u>Assignment for the Self-Driving Car topic</u>: Research and prepare a paper and Self-Driving Cars. Cite at least 3 reputable sources and analyze the characterizations. Compare and contrast to what has been stated in this book.

c) <u>Assignment for a Business topic</u>: Research and prepare a paper and a presentation on businesses and advanced technology. What is hot, and what is not? Cite at least 3 reputable sources. Compare and contrast to the depictions in this book.

d) <u>Assignment to do a Startup:</u> Have the students prepare a paper about how they might startup a business in this realm. They must submit a sound Business Plan for the startup. They could also be asked to present their Business Plan and so should also have a presentation deck to coincide with it.

You can certainly adjust the aforementioned assignments to fit to your particular needs and the class structure. You'll notice that I ask for 3 reputable cited sources for the paper writing based assignments. I usually steer students toward "reputable" publications, since otherwise they will cite some oddball source that has no credentials other than that they happened to write something and post it onto the Internet. You can define "reputable" in whatever way you prefer, for example some faculty think Wikipedia is not reputable while others believe it is reputable and allow students to cite it.

The reason that I usually ask for at least 3 citations is that if the student only does one or two citations they usually settle on whatever they happened to find the fastest. By requiring three citations, it usually seems to force them to look around, explore, and end-up probably finding five or more, and then whittling it down to 3 that they will actually use.

I have not specified the length of their papers, and leave that to you to tell the students what you prefer. For each of those assignments, you could end-up with a short one to two pager, or you could do a dissertation length paper. Base the length on whatever best fits for your class, and the credit amount of the assignment within the context of the other grading metrics you'll be using for the class.

I mention in the assignments that they are to do a paper and prepare a presentation. I usually try to get students to present their work. This is a good practice for what they will do in the business world. Most of the time, they will be required to prepare an analysis and present it. If you don't have the class time or inclination to have the students present, then you can of course cut out the aspect of them putting together a presentation.

If you want to point students toward highly ranked journals in AI, here's a list of the top journals as reported by *various citation counts sources* (this list changes year to year):

- o   Communications of the ACM
- o   Artificial Intelligence
- o   Cognitive Science
- o   IEEE Transactions on Pattern Analysis and Machine Intelligence
- o   Foundations and Trends in Machine Learning
- o   Journal of Memory and Language
- o   Cognitive Psychology
- o   Neural Networks
- o   IEEE Transactions on Neural Networks and Learning Systems
- o   IEEE Intelligent Systems
- o   Knowledge-based Systems

GUIDE TO USING THE CHAPTERS

For each of the chapters, I provide next some various ways to use the chapter material. You can assign the tasks as individual homework assignments, or the tasks can be used with team projects for the class. You can easily layout a series of assignments, such as indicating that the students are to do item "a" below for say Chapter 1, then "b" for the next chapter of the book, and so on.

a) What is the main point of the chapter and describe in your own words the significance of the topic,

b) Identify at least two aspects in the chapter that you agree with, and support your concurrence by providing at least one other outside researched item as support; make sure to explain your basis for disagreeing with the aspects,

c) Identify at least two aspects in the chapter that you disagree with, and support your disagreement by providing at least one other outside researched item as support; make sure to explain your basis for disagreeing with the aspects,

d) Find an aspect that was not covered in the chapter, doing so by conducting outside research, and then explain how that aspect ties into the chapter and what significance it brings to the topic,

e) Interview a specialist in industry about the topic of the chapter, collect from them their thoughts and opinions, and readdress the chapter by citing your source and how they compared and contrasted to the material,

f) Interview a relevant academic professor or researcher in a college or university about the topic of the chapter, collect from them their thoughts and opinions, and readdress the chapter by citing your source and how they compared and contrasted to the material,

g) Try to update a chapter by finding out the latest on the topic, and ascertain whether the issue or topic has now been solved or whether it is still being addressed, explain what you come up with.

The above are all ways in which you can get the students of your class involved in considering the material of a given chapter. You could mix things up by having one of those above assignments per each week, covering the chapters over the course of the semester or quarter.

As a reminder, here are the chapters of the book and you can select whichever chapters you find most valued for your particular class:

<u>Chapter Title</u>

Companion Book By This Author

Advances in AI and Autonomous Vehicles: Cybernetic Self-Driving Cars

Practical Advances in Artificial Intelligence (AI) and Machine Learning

by

Dr. Lance B. Eliot, MBA, PhD

Chapter Title

This title is available via Amazon and other book sellers

<u>Companion Book By This Author</u>

Self-Driving Cars:
"The Mother of All AI Projects"

by Dr. Lance B. Eliot, MBA, PhD

<u>Chapter Title</u>

This title is available via Amazon and other book sellers

Companion Book By This Author

Innovation and Thought Leadership on Self-Driving Driverless Cars

by Dr. Lance B. Eliot, MBA, PhD

This title is available via Amazon and other book sellers

Companion Book By This Author

New Advances in AI Autonomous Driverless Cars Self-Driving Cars

by Dr. Lance B. Eliot, MBA, PhD

This title is available via Amazon and other book sellers

Companion Book By This Author

Introduction to
Driverless Self-Driving Cars

by Dr. Lance B. Eliot, MBA, PhD

This title is available via Amazon and other book sellers

Companion Book By This Author
Autonomous Vehicle Driverless Self-Driving Cars and Artificial Intelligence
by Dr. Lance B. Eliot, MBA, PhD

This title is available via Amazon and other book sellers

Companion Book By This Author

Transformative Artificial Intelligence Driverless Self-Driving Cars

by Dr. Lance B. Eliot, MBA, PhD

This title is available via Amazon and other book sellers

<u>Companion Book By This Author</u>

Disruptive Artificial Intelligence and Driverless Self-Driving Cars

by Dr. Lance B. Eliot, MBA, PhD

<u>Chapter Title</u>

This title is available via Amazon and other book sellers

Companion Book By This Author

State-of-the-Art
AI Driverless Self-Driving Cars

by Dr. Lance B. Eliot, MBA, PhD

<u>Chapter Title</u>

1 Eliot Framework for AI Self-Driving Cars

2 Versioning and Self-Driving Cars

3 Towing and Self-Driving Cars

4 Driving Styles and Self-Driving Cars

5 Bicyclists and Self-Driving Vehicles

6 Back-up Cams and Self-Driving Cars

7 Traffic Mix and Self-Driving Cars

8 Hot-Car Deaths and Self-Driving Cars

9 Machine Learning Performance and Self-Driving Cars

10 Sensory Illusions and Self-Driving Cars

11 Federated Machine Learning and Self-Driving Cars

12 Irreproducibility and Self-Driving Cars

13 In-Car Deliveries and Self-Driving Cars

This title is available via Amazon and other book sellers

<u>Companion Book By This Author</u>

Top Trends in
AI Self-Driving Cars

by Dr. Lance B. Eliot, MBA, PhD

<u>Chapter Title</u>

This title is available via Amazon and other book sellers

<u>Companion Book By This Author</u>

AI Innovations and Self-Driving Cars

by Dr. Lance B. Eliot, MBA, PhD

This title is available via Amazon and other book sellers

Companion Book By This Author

Crucial Advances for AI Self-Driving Cars

by Dr. Lance B. Eliot, MBA, PhD

<u>Chapter Title</u>

This title is available via Amazon and other book sellers

Companion Book By This Author

Sociotechnical Insights and AI Driverless Cars

by Dr. Lance B. Eliot, MBA, PhD

Chapter Title

This title is available via Amazon and other book sellers

Companion Book By This Author

Pioneering Advances for
AI Driverless Cars

by Dr. Lance B. Eliot, MBA, PhD

This title is available via Amazon and other book sellers

Companion Book By This Author

Leading Edge Trends for AI Driverless Cars

by Dr. Lance B. Eliot, MBA, PhD

This title is available via Amazon and other book sellers

Companion Book By This Author

The Cutting Edge of AI Autonomous Cars

by Dr. Lance B. Eliot, MBA, PhD

This title is available via Amazon and other book sellers

Companion Book By This Author

The Next Wave of
AI Self-Driving Cars

by Dr. Lance B. Eliot, MBA, PhD

<u>Chapter Title</u>

This title is available via Amazon and other book sellers

Companion Book By This Author

Revolutionary Innovations of
AI Self-Driving Cars

by Dr. Lance B. Eliot, MBA, PhD

Chapter Title

This title is available via Amazon and other book sellers

Companion Book By This Author

AI Self-Driving Cars
Breakthroughs

by Dr. Lance B. Eliot, MBA, PhD

Chapter Title

1   Eliot Framework for AI Self-Driving Cars

2   Off-Roading and AI Self-Driving Cars

3   Paralleling Vehicles and AI Self-Driving Cars

4   Dementia Drivers and AI Self-Driving Cars

5   Augmented Realty (AR) and AI Self-Driving Cars

6   Sleeping Inside an AI Self-Driving Car

7   Prevalence Detection and AI Self-Driving Cars

8   Super-Intelligent AI and AI Self-Driving Cars

9   Car Caravans and AI Self-Driving Cars

This title is available via Amazon and other book sellers

Companion Book By This Author

***Trailblazing Trends for*
AI Self-Driving Cars**

by Dr. Lance B. Eliot, MBA, PhD

This title is available via Amazon and other book sellers

Companion Book By This Author

Ingenious Strides for **AI Driverless Cars**

by Dr. Lance B. Eliot, MBA, PhD

<u>Chapter Title</u>

This title is available via Amazon and other book sellers

Companion Book By This Author

AI Self-Driving Cars Inventiveness

by Dr. Lance B. Eliot, MBA, PhD

This title is available via Amazon and other book sellers

Companion Book By This Author

Visionary Secrets of AI Driverless Cars

by Dr. Lance B. Eliot, MBA, PhD

<u>Chapter Title</u>

This title is available via Amazon and other book sellers

Companion Book By This Author

Spearheading
AI Self-Driving Cars

by Dr. Lance B. Eliot, MBA, PhD

This title is available via Amazon and other book sellers

ABOUT THE AUTHOR

Dr. Lance B. Eliot, MBA, PhD is the CEO of Techbruim, Inc. and Executive Director of the Cybernetic AI Self-Driving Car Institute, and has over twenty years of industry experience including serving as a corporate officer in a billion dollar firm and was a partner in a major executive services firm. He is also a serial entrepreneur having founded, ran, and sold several high-tech related businesses. He previously hosted the popular radio show *Technotrends* that was also available on American Airlines flights via their in-flight audio program. Author or co-author of a dozen books and over 400 articles, he has made appearances on CNN, and has been a frequent speaker at industry conferences.

A former professor at the University of Southern California (USC), he founded and led an innovative research lab on Artificial Intelligence in Business. Known as the "AI Insider" his writings on AI advances and trends has been widely read and cited. He also previously served on the faculty of the University of California Los Angeles (UCLA), and was a visiting professor at other major universities. He was elected to the International Board of the Society for Information Management (SIM), a prestigious association of over 3,000 high-tech executives worldwide.

He has performed extensive community service, including serving as Senior Science Adviser to the Vice Chair of the Congressional Committee on Science & Technology. He has served on the Board of the OC Science & Engineering Fair (OCSEF), where he is also has been a Grand Sweepstakes judge, and likewise served as a judge for the Intel International SEF (ISEF). He served as the Vice Chair of the Association for Computing Machinery (ACM) Chapter, a prestigious association of computer scientists. Dr. Eliot has been a shark tank judge for the USC Mark Stevens Center for Innovation on start-up pitch competitions, and served as a mentor for several incubators and accelerators in Silicon Valley and Silicon Beach. He served on several Boards and Committees at USC, including having served on the Marshall Alumni Association (MAA) Board in Southern California.

Dr. Eliot holds a PhD from USC, MBA, and Bachelor's in Computer Science, and earned the CDP, CCP, CSP, CDE, and CISA certifications. Born and raised in Southern California, and having traveled and lived internationally, he enjoys scuba diving, surfing, and sailing.

ADDENDUM

Spearheading
AI Self-Driving Cars

Practical Advances in Artificial Intelligence (AI)
and Machine Learning

By
Dr. Lance B. Eliot, MBA, PhD

For supplemental materials of this book, visit:
www.ai-selfdriving-cars.guru

For special orders of this book, contact:
LBE Press Publishing
Email: LBE.Press.Publishing@gmail.com